Where Have All The Camel Toes Gone?

Keyz Karanza

Where Have All The Camel Toes Gone?

Published by
Awful Show Press
Waynesburg, PA 15370

Copyright © 2009 Awful Show Press. All rights reserved.

ISBN 978-0-557-17416-4

No portion of this book may be reproduced, in whole or in part, or transmitted in any form, electronic or mechanical including photocopying, recording and information storage and retrieval, without the prior written permission of publisher.

First Printing: March 2010

 is a trademark under exclusive license to Awful Show Press.

ACKNOWLEGEMENTS

Thanks to my family, for understanding how important it is for me to be myself, even though they thought I was completely insane.

Thanks to my friends, for laughing at my humor when they **knew** I was completely insane.

Thanks to The Awful Show (http://awfulshow.com) for giving me an outlet for my insanity.

Thanks to the late George Carlin, without whom I would have never found my inner lunatic.

SPECIAL PROPS TO...

"The Fuse Was Too Cold"
http://thefusewastoocold.blogspot.com

Scrub Club Records
http://scrubclubrecords.com/9/

Foxy Veronica's Peach Pies
http://www.myspace.com/foxyveronica

and of course...

The Awful Show
http://awfulshow.com/

FOREWORD

It's just a guess, but I think the answer to the question on the cover of this book is...Walmart. And not sexy ones either. Seems the only women wearing spandex these days are ones that have no business doing it. Massive women with enormous asses that push the material to its limits. Now that I think of it, maybe they aren't even wearing actual spandex. Maybe they were wearing some other material and as it stretched beyond it's natural limit, the material polymerized into spandex. It's just a theory.

Anyway, when Nerraux asked if he could call me to make an appearance on Show #2, the thought that I would be a regular part of The Awful Show for the next three and a half years and counting had not even come close to the vicinity in the region of crossing my mind. It has been quite a ride.

I'll admit that when the notion of "Snacks" came along, I was very pleased. While I don't have anything against the structure of the regular Friday shows, it can be stifling at times. The Snack concept lifted that structure completely and gave all of us a chance to spread our wings. And with my wings spread, I've taken flight and generally shit on everything under the sun.

Since the Snacks have begun, mine has taken a number of different forms, such as Saturday Night SYN (which was way, WAY more work than it was worth in the end) and He Said, She Said Movie Reviews (which fizzled out, mainly due to it being difficult to rely on so many people for material every week), but the snacks that have always been closest to my heart are the "Classics". The ranting, raving, lunatic stream of consciousness that so many have laughed themselves to incontinence at.

It feels great using this opportunity to put that same type of material in a form that can be taken anywhere, and that doesn't rely on batteries. While I haven't recorded a classic snack in some time, that doesn't mean I haven't been keeping track of my bizarre notions in one form or another. Some stuff is scribbled in notebooks. Much of it is in my microcassette recorder. All of it, however, will be in this book.

I hope you all get as much enjoyment out of reading this as you did from the audio recordings. And if you didn't enjoy my audio recordings, then fuck you.

Where Have All The Camel Toes Gone?

BLIND EYES

I used to be a pretty avid fan of Hollywood Squares. Before Comcast took away my Game Show Network that is. One of the contestants that they had on was a blind guy. Typically, blind people wear sunglasses, but in this case he wasn't. And he had those kinds of eyes where one is looking straight ahead and the other is looking into the rafters or staring at the Big Dipper or some shit. If that wasn't bad enough, his eyes were also constantly moving around! I'm trying to watch the show and here's Ray Charles with these fucking crazy googly eyes making me sick. I don't need to see that shit! Put the goddamn sunglasses on! I almost lost my fucking lunch watching this blind freak!

And what the fuck do his eyes need to be rolling all over the place for anyway. The son of a bitch isn't going to be able to see no matter which fucking way he looks! Here's a new law I want to see put in place. Any time blind people are in public, they're required to wear sunglasses. The next blind prick I see without sunglasses is getting my cookies tossed all over them. Fucking disgusting!

PRISON FOR PARIS

Some time ago, the nation's favorite claptrap, Paris Hilton, was busted for drunk driving. She was taken to a county jail in Los Angeles, and I guess she was none to happy about it. Fuck her! I think what they should have done was stripped her ass naked, and thrown her into general population with nothing but KY Jelly and PCP. Let those convicts anal rape that pig for about a week; week and a half perhaps. Knock that snooty cunt down a couple hundred pegs.

RAISIN TARD CRUNCH

I made a decision a couple of years ago to return to watching movies on DVD and commercial-free Simpsons and Family Guy. The main reason for doing this was because of the commercials. My blood pressure must have climbed 10 points every time a commercial came on. A good deal of this book is dedicated to the all-mighty shit stew known as advertising. I want to warm up slowly so I'll pick a few of the more annoying ones to start.

Here's the scene: 3 jackoffs sitting around eating Raisin Bran Crunch and waxing philosophic. The first two wastes of hemoglobin are debating back and forth about the most important element of the cereal, between the raisins and the crunch clusters. After going round and round for what seems like a fucking decade, the third fucktard chimes in with something completely idiotic and offbeat. When he does, the first two look at him like he's giving birth to a baby walrus nasally.

News Flash! All three of you fucking imbeciles deserve to be beaten to death with a giant dildo! You're sitting around debating about a fucking breakfast cereal! Do the world a favor. Go to your local hardware store, buy a box of rat poison, sprinkle it liberally on that shitty cereal and **then** eat it! You bunch of shitgasms! You're sucking the intelligence out of people every time your ugly baboon-ass faces are on the TV screen! Kill yourselves, you fucking colostomy bags! Jesus!

Oh, and by the way, I'm not really sure what a shitgasm is. It just sounded good at the time. I guess it would be some manner of orgasm experienced while taking a shit. Either that or shitting while having an orgasm. It would seem the latter would leave much more cleaning to do. Eww!

STAY IN YOUR OWN STATE!

I've talked at length on the show about my hatred for out-of-state drivers. But this is it. I've been pushed to the limit! You motherfuckers have been warned before! Now, the time has come to start killing you sons-of-bitches! You know who you are! You fucking Ohio drivers that drive in Pennsylvania! From now on, you cocksuckers are going to start being killed! It's genocide time! If you're driving in Pennsylvania with an Ohio license plate, you're targeted, motherfucker! No warnings. None of this 3-strikes-and-your-out shit. This *is* your fucking warning right here! Stay in your own fucking state or you will **die**! And if you're moving to Pennsylvania from Ohio, get your plates changed *before* you cross the border. If you don't, you'll be executed just like the rest! And you West Virginians who don't know how to use a fucking turn signal, you ball sacks are next! The Keystone State is now off limits to all you pricks!

And don't even get me going on you Ontario drivers! I can't drive 5 miles on the interstate without seeing some ass crack who thinks curling is a real sport. What the fuck is that about?? Oh, wait; let me rephrase that so you Canuck fucks can understand it. What the fuck is that **aboot**?? Like goddamn locusts, you moose fuckers just swarmed right in to

Pennsylvania! Ontario, that isn't even in this country for fuck's sake! Show me a green card or die, you north-Mexican piece of shit! Next time you cross the border is going to be in a fucking body bag!

There's only one thing worse than a Ohioan driving a Ford. That's an Ontarian driving a Toyota. I'm working on embroidering that on a pillow.

GO (SUCK MY) MEAT!

Here's another group of commercials that rubbed me the wrong way. Hillshire Farm decided to come out with this series of ads that revolve around the phrase "Go Meat"! I don't know whom the drunken burrito fart that came up with that idea was, but someone got paid for it. There was one that was actually tolerable. Two chicks eating lunch. One is having a Hillshire Farm chicken salad. And when she's shaking the chicken bits out of the package, you hear the chanting "Go Meat" crowd. And at the very end, one of the girls goes "Wooo"! I get a mild chuckle out of that. Probably because she's cute and I have a much higher tolerance for commercials that feature cute chicks.

But there was another that takes place in an office. And as one of the broads is making a salad, the people in the cubicles around her are doing the chanting. As I watched this commercial, I wanted nothing more than to load a van up with C-4, drive it into the basement and set it off. Then sit back with a smile as the building full of schmucks came crashing down. And then the fuckers can cheer about their splattered and dismembered body parts. There's one butt ugly freak in that commercial with bushy hair and glasses. That cocksucker had me asking, "What tardbeast shit that out"?!? I couldn't figure out what the fuck it was supposed to be. It looked like Pat (an old Julia Sweeney character from Saturday Night Live), only much more hideous. It was the most disgusting pile of protoplasm I had ever seen! This will give you a little information about me as a person: When I see something like that, some nasty fucking turd who has no business showing their face on television, my instinct is to hunt it down and beat it to death. For no other reason than the fact that it exists!

And what the fuck is the deal with that chant anyway? *You hungry, you hungry, yo mama said you hungry!* How about this: the next one of you buckets of diarrhea to even mentions my mother get their intestines removed with a rusty ice cream scoop!

Here's a technological advance that's way overdue. Have a button on the TV remote that kills everybody on the screen. And I'm not talking about the characters and using CGI or anything like that to do it. I'm talking about having an actual database of the actors and actresses (yes, I do still make the distinction. The concept of a female actor is just fucking retarded), use satellite and GPS tracking to hunt them down wherever they are, and with an onboard plasma cannon (or whatever technology happens to be available) blast them into a million little bloody pieces. My philosophy: They read the script and still took the job, so they knew the risk involved!

And that goes for anyone in any commercial. You fuckers have been warned.

POLI-DICKS

During the most recent primaries, I heard on the radio that there were people marching around with signs and that I should drive carefully because I don't want to hit any of them. And I couldn't help but think, "I don't?!? Who the fuck do you think you're talking to??" Maybe it's just me but I actually think the world would benefit from turning these political-minded jackoffs into road pizza.

A.I. (ANIMAL INTELLIGENCE) – PART 1

I've given this a lot of thought and I've come to the conclusion that subhuman animals are telepathic. They have to be. It would certainly explain a lot of things. When animals do something that humans wouldn't ever think to do, we chalk it up to instinct. But that's pretty lame when you think about it. It's just about as lame as the whole "God's Will" thing explaining phenomena that can't be immediately explained. At least until science has a chance, but you know how impatient religious people are.

Plus the whole instinct argument has a fatal flaw: Humans don't have any. Why not? Are we not animals at our roots? I know what you're going to say: "Well, why aren't we telepathic"? Simply put, we don't need to be. Our ability to communicate intelligently has fulfilled and replaced any need to communicate telepathically. Animals can only make primitive sounds. And while I'm not saying we need instincts, it sure would be helpful if we had them! At least a few anyway. The whole toilet-training thing comes to mind. Nasty!

But back to my point of animals being telepathic. I think that animals have an actual language. I don't mean meow-tweet-woof. I'm referring to a language much like humans use. But since they don't have the ability to employ it verbally like us, they communicate by thoughts. Look at a flock of birds. They can be flying in one direction, then in a split second fly in a completely different one. And not just one bird. The whole flock! Moving like they're a single entity. Can you imagine humans doing that? Well, we do. Watch an Army unit doing drills. Everyone moves in unison, but at the leader's command. If you put a gag on him and whispered for one guy to face left, he would be the only one doing it. The others would eventually turn, but not like the flock of birds. It's as if the whole flock can read the lead bird's mind. Isn't it?

Makes me wonder if we're so fucking superior to animals after all.

FINGER LICKIN' BAD

I can't believe I'm the only one to notice that ads for Kentucky Fried Chicken (or KFC for you abbreviphiliacs) are getting worse all the time. Someone has to be able to back me up on this.

First and foremost, what would possess the marketing spooge in this company to adopt the song "Sweet Home Alabama" as their theme? Did I miss something? Did they relocate? Did the name change to Alabama Fried Chicken when I wasn't looking and they decided not to use the abbreviation AFC because it's already an NFL conference? Here's an abbreviation for you: PPP. Piss Poor Planning.

But the whole theme music deal is just the tip of the iceberg. For the record, this is about as racially tolerant as I get, so enjoy it. There was a commercial in the not too distant past where a black guy is eating KFC for lunch and a white guy comes up looking for a piece. He asks for a leg. The black guy says, "That's my favorite". So he asks for a wing. Black guy says, "That's my other favorite". And this goes on and on until it's clear that all of the chicken is the black guy's favorite. At the time, I dismissed this as just a slight oversight by the commercial writers. So a week or so later, another commercial comes out that has a different black guy eating KFC and a different white guy eating a burger. And I think *what the fuck*?!? Is this the direction the campaign is going?? Is the marketing department stoned or are they just so oblivious that they have no idea they're branding the company as the official food provider of David fucking Duke?

So I'll be keeping an eye on them, but don't be surprised when you see the next commercial with 2 families involved. Both of them at a picnic. The camera pans over the white guy's table and shows macaroni salad, corn on the cob, burgers and dogs. Standard picnic fare. Then they slide over to the black table, and surrounding the big bucket of KFC in the middle of the table, you see it all! Watermelon, chitlins, grits, collard greens, Mad Dog 20/20 and malt liquor.

Piss poor planning. And did you notice how PPP resembles another abbreviation so well? Like KKK?

BIG BROTHER, WHITE COURTESY PHONE

Get this shit! A few years back Google filed a patent for some in-game advertising technology. An ability of this technology would be to track in-game behaviors so they can evaluate an individual's purchasing tendencies.

What...the...fuck!!!

Here are a few more details of this 1984-esque situation. The details of the patent stated that Google would be able to monitor gamers playing on any console that hooks up to the Internet, including the PS3, the Xbox 360 and the Nintendo Wii. It states that user dialog, as well as user play may be used to characterize the user. Here's the fun part. Google believes that this information will allow for companies to tailor in-game advertising to make it more relevant to the user.

Alright. Hit the pause button, right fucking there.

In-game advertising. Let's look a little closer at that. When you go on pages and sites that have 'free games', naturally it's to be expected that in order to pay to make and host the games, there's going to be advertising. That's fine. You get to play for free and in exchange they get to bombard you with advertisements for web business that will hook you up with your high school sweetheart and track down your credit score. Advertising like this, I've developed the ability to ignore. That is what Firefox doesn't block from the get go. The same principle goes true for any kind of 'free' entertainment, including network television and radio. Advertising is expected. It's a basic need to pay the bills.

However, when I shell out $50-$60 bucks for a game, one that in material worth lies somewhere between a paper clip and a can of Shasta, and I still have to put up with advertisements, that's some serious, Grade-A, blue ribbon bullshit! And I'm not even concerned with Dodge putting a logo on a car in a NASCAR game. Or billboards along the back wall of stadiums in a baseball game. But when you're talking about custom-crafted advertising, I get ready to power down the system, throw it on the coffee table and use it to prop my feet up. The last thing I need is to be enjoying a game of Ghost Recon, use a bandage power up and see an ad for Tampax pop up on the screen. Likewise I have no desire to be playing Earthworm Jim XVII, use the sonic fart blaster, and see a pitch for Beano go dancing across the screen!

I wish to make it known that if these marketing semen stains start putting this shit in ANY game that I spend good money for, I'm putting all my time into the bootleg software business! I'll team up with a guy who can install mod chips into game systems, and we will sell the systems complete with every game available, ripped and backed up for no more than the cost of the blank disks. Let's see what kind of profit Google can project when they put advertisements in software that **no one is paying for**!!

Not to be a total outlaw in this matter, there's one benefit. If I'm fragging n00bs in Quake, and the game decides it wants to advertise The Church of Latter Day Saints by sending a guy across with a sandwich board, I'll take great pleasure in blowing his head off, running over and fucking the corpse! Or at least wiggling the joystick to make it look like I'm fucking it.

SENSITIVE EYES

People are way too touchy these days. A while back I was at the optometrist. To make it clear, I have piss poor vision. When I don't have my glasses on, the doctor will tell me to read the first line of the chart. I say, "What chart?" They're really fucking horrible. When I talked to him, he told me I was a candidate for laser eye correction. He said it was an elective surgery. I replied to him: "Candidate? Elective? What the fuck is this? An eye exam or Meet the Press"?? He gets all nervous and tells me to settle down because there are children in the waiting room. I told him "It isn't my fault their slut mothers couldn't keep their fucking legs closed". He has the nerve to tell me to leave. People need to lighten up, seriously.

DON'T LET NISSAN GO DOWN ON ME

Driving home from work the other day, I got behind a Nissan Murano. This got my ever-calculating brain thinking. I wondered if the person driving was a woman named Alyssa. If it was, it would have been Alyssa's Murano! Get it? Hahahahah! Alyssa Milano...Murano! Hahah...hah...??

Well, **fuck you**! It was funny at the time!!

YOU SAY YOU WANT A RAV-OLUTION

I think one of the stupidest, most grating names for a vehicle would be the Toyota RAV. I don't even know why. It's just one of those names that fills me with loathing and spite, and I want to stick my head out of the window yelling "RAV! RAV!" mocking the driver like a 6-year-old kid. I could never figure that type of thing out. I think everyone has a set of words they hate. Maybe they don't have the same degree of psychotic response to them as I do, but still...Fucking RAV! It wouldn't be nearly as stupid to me if it was the Toyota Rave. To me that sounds like a reasonably cool name for a car.

Someone told me it was an initialism for "Recreational Active Vehicle". Ok, fine. But as opposed to what? A recreational DORMANT vehicle?? That would make sense since it's a Toyota. A vehicle that doesn't go anywhere. But doesn't the word 'vehicle' already imply it's ability to go from one place to another, in other words, that it's ACTIVE and not stationary?? So right there, the initialism is ridiculous. But the other thing about it is, if it's an initialism, why is it pronounced like a word? I live in the USA, but I don't go around saying I live in "ooh-sah"! How many people do you know that own an SUV and say "I'm going down to Florida in my suv" instead of pronouncing it "ess-you-vee".

While I was at it though, I looked up some other translations of the RAV initialism. One of them was "Risk Assessment Value". That's a good one, considering you're risking you life every time you get behind the wheel of one of those pieces of shit. "Restricted AVailablity". That one doesn't make a whole lot of sense, because they unfortunately aren't restricted enough. I see those fucking things all over the road when I venture out into the general public. "Real-time Audio/Video" was another. It's a bit cryptic, but if you read between the lines, you can figure out that you're better off staying home and watching TV instead of getting into one. And then there was my favorite: "Random Acts of Vandalism" or "Random Acts of Violence". Either of these is appropriate seeing as I'm inspired to both of them when I see one of these shitboxes. Kill the driver, trash the car. Sounds like a plan to me.

Though as vandalism inspiring as a RAV is to me, it can't hold a candle to a Scion XB. First of all, Scion is the same as Toyota. Same fucking rice-burner piece of shit, different name! But the XB...how is it best described? I would call it a shoebox with wheels. This is by far the pimple-ass-ugliest thing to ever pollute the streets. It's the kind of vehicle that can give one the overwhelming urge of running it straight into a concrete divider! It doesn't matter if you're on a moped! You still think it's worth taking a shot at just to disable it! God dammit! Just thinking about it makes me want to destroy something! And if you happen to be one of the drivers of this vehicle, I offer no apologies whatsoever!! You're a retched, buoyant turd floating in the toilet of life, and your mother should have had a fucking **miscarriage**!!!

Anyway...Not to stray too far from the subject of abbreviation. This one is pretty easy. Scion, much like RAV, is an abbreviation. A lot of people don't know that; it isn't common knowledge, but I'll go ahead and let the cat out of the bag on this one. Not that I carry a cat around in a bag. Where the hell did a saying like that...fuck! Keyz! Focus! Okay, yes. Scion is an abbreviation. It stands for "Spoiled Children Is Our Niggers"! Because, when you take a close look at these things, whom do you see driving them? Spoiled, silver-spoon-chomping, over-privileged little shit bastards! The little fucks who didn't even pay for the thing because mommy and daddy gave it to them for their 16th birthday!!! Little Ass Monkey Bitch **Piss Motherfuckers!!!!!!**

Fuck it! I'm done with this topic. I need a drink.

WE'LL BE BACK IN TWO AND TWO

It has been a while since I've watched network television, but I remember several other commercials that played a big part in my departure from that.

There was a series of commercials from 21st Century Insurance. The general notion behind the commercial was "21st Century drivers are just like you". The first commercial was this fucking idiot who puts his gay little purse on the roof and forgets it's there as he drives through town. And I don't call it a man bag, soft briefcase or portfolio. If it doesn't appear rectangular from all 3 views, it's a fucking purse!

Next up they have this dumb cunt that can't find her car. To be clear, she's parked outside of an office building or small business. It isn't like she's parked outside of Walmart the day after Thanksgiving. There are two, maybe three-dozen cars in the lot at the time. Not a whole lot to choose from. And here she's wandering around like a retard on smack looking for a car she parked herself!

Lastly, there's this jackoff who is coming out of a parking garage and looking everywhere except up his own ass for the ticket. At least I'm guessing he didn't look up there. I don't know; they may have edited it out. And the fucking thing is hanging out of his visor, right in front of his face! Then when he grabs the thing, it slips out of his fingers like they're covered with KY jelly. They probably were. He had that type of look to him. Then the dickhead opens the door right into a pole.

I'm sure there were more stupid jackoff commercials like that in circulation. Those were just the three I remember. But the bottom line: These retards think I'm going to buy insurance from **them**?!? I'm not that comfortable with the fact that these extra-chromosome laden assholes even survived childbirth! The last thing I'm going to do is give them money!! And what's even more insulting is their claim that I'm a driver just like them! I want to tie these motherfuckers to a steel table and grind their genitals off with a citrus zester for a comment like that! Cocksuckers!

Another commercial that was not so insulting as it was just a little disturbing was for Serenity. They're the ones who make those snatch pads. I don't know what they're actually called. Something like feminine wetness incontinence protection or some shit. I just call them snatch pads. It's a lot easier. And they had this CGI deal that I suppose was some type of springtime freshness analogy or something. But they showed these flowers and all the petals of the flowers were these snatch pads! Jesus, is that fucked up! What do you do with a flower? You put your nose in it and smell it, right? I can only assume that whoever wrote this commercial is some kind of sick-ass pad sniffer! But at least the pads were clean. It was like a daisy with white petals. I guess I should be happy it wasn't a dandelion or a rose!

There was a rather puzzling commercial series you might have seen: Lunesta. I have a hard time following commercials these days but from what I can gather, Lunesta is a radioactive butterfly that flutters around from house to house putting people to sleep. I haven't yet figured out if the advertisement is for a sci-fi movie or for some unmentioned exterminator.

The next line of promotionals, I have a hard time insulting, because I happen to like a lot of their adverts: Geico. Their commercials with the cavemen and the little gecko with the English accent have amused me on numerous occasions. However some of what I refer to as their 'freelance' scenarios have driven me to shaking the TV in rage from time to time. In a handful of them, the general message is "there are better things you can be doing with 15 minutes online". One of them shows a web video of these two guys charging at each other holding flimsy dorm room mattresses and colliding, sort of like a coed joust. I enjoyed that one! Every time I saw it, I would say "God! That looks like fun"! But as amusing as that one was, there was a yang to its yin.

The other showed a web video of what appears to be the ugliest, most nauseating piece of human flotsam on the planet, sitting in front of his webcam and acting like a complete and total fucking retard. This anal loaf is sticking his retched, slimy tongue out at the camera. And it looks like his tongue is covered with gay cum. Probably is. He appeared to be the type who does nothing but suck cock 24-7. He's tucking his chin way down under giving himself another 30 chins and making noises like a barnyard full of animals getting fucked in the ass! By him, most likely. I made an oath to myself that if I ever saw this walking diarrhea-filled condom, I'll beat him to fucking death! As I said before, for no other reason than its very existence! And when the police are pulling me away from his pulverized corpse, I'll openly blame it on Geico, because they're the ones who put him on TV! With that video as 'Exhibit A', there won't be a fucking court in the country that blames me for doing it.

Now that I think of it, there was one caveman commercial that bothered me. It was set up like one of those news programs where they have the host at the studio and they have a video feed with someone else in a different place. What I never got about that: they put the money and effort to send a whole video crew out to set up a live remote with someone, as opposed to just sending the guy a 2-way plane ticket. Maybe it's not for me to understand. It must be a strange industry. So anyway, they have a man and woman newscaster in the one window and the caveman in the other. So this douchebag and this cunt are giving the caveman the hardest time. They're talking down to him like a child, really discounting his whole objection to the "so easy a caveman can do it" slogan, and they continue to give him shit through the whole commercial.

I would have liked, in a follow-up commercial, for him to really bring that stereotype to life. Say you have the news cocks interviewing another poor soul. Then you hear a door being ripped off the hinges and the next thing you see is the caveman going fucking feral on them, just like the Cro-Magnon he really is! He tears over to the asshole and just starts bashing the fuck out of him with a club, blood and brains shooting everywhere. Then he runs over to the twat (who by now is screaming herself mute), grabs her from behind, rips off her skirt and panties and begins to rape the shit out of her, all the while drawing pictographs on her back in the asshole's blood. While that would be a little too hardcore for a mainstream audience, it would certainly be a refreshing taste of reality in advertising. Go Caveman! It's your birthday!

There have just been so many commercials deserving of a Keyz-style caning. A Keyzing. Ooh, there we go! I'm declaring that as a new term. A definition for that? Let's see...verb, to ridicule common stupidity with twisted yet accurate logic. There you have it. Call Webster up and make sure that goes in his next edition. Not Emmanuel Lewis! The *other* Webster. The dictionary guy.

There was one more insurance commercial I saw for Progressive a while ago. Some dipshit is talking about getting car insurance, all the while cleaning up a mess of cheesy poofs all over the living room. It looked like a fucking bag of them had exploded. He mentions that Progressive gives you the rates of other competitors and closes with "that type of honesty is refreshing". Right after that, in comes this parade of rug rats. He grabs the last one who has cheesy poof residue all over his face, looks him in the eye and asks "Did you have anything to do with this?" pointing at the mess, to which the little brat replies "No". So the guy lets the prepubescent dork run off on his way. Are you fucking kidding me?? It's obvious this kid is a little fucking liar, and he just let him run right off? Fuck that shit! He should have beat the little bastard! Scream at him "Don't you ever fucking lie to me again, you little shit"! Start smacking him around, throw him face down on the couch and thrash his ass with the fucking laptop! Punishment, god damn it! What the fuck is wrong with people that they have stopped punishing their children?? That's why these little fucks misbehave so much! Beat the child, just like you and I were beaten when we were children! It's a tried-and-true formula for behavioral control and today's pussy-ass parents are letting it slip away! And if Child Services comes and takes the child away, at least you don't have to worry about fucking cheesy poofs all over the living room anymore. Problem solved.

A BIRD IN THE HAND

The English language can be so much fun sometimes. I was thinking about this. Say one day we decided to eat rooster as commonly as we eat chicken. Perhaps it would be more of a delicacy. I may have to give Frank Perdue a call and see if that would be a possibility. But say they started packaging rooster along with the usual chicken. And in an effort to offer a variety of taste options, they decided to do various marinades and smoke flavorings like they do with turkey and ham. Do you realize that it would be possible to take a job as a professional cock smoker?

Oh, wait. That title has already been taken. The other term for it is "politician".

A SCROTUM BY ANY OTHER NAME

Foreign languages have always, to me, been nothing but a big pain in the ass. But every so often, they can prove themselves to be quite humorous. In the first half of the 1800s, there was a French novelist and playwright by the name of Honoré Balzac. His last name is funny enough. Any time your last name is pronounced almost like your nut bag, there are great guffaws to be had. However, taking someone with a French name and having him announced in a different country could be downright sidesplitting. Imagine Honoré takes a trip to Germany to promote his latest book. When he was arriving at a formal location, would he not have been announced as "Herr Balzac"?? If I was the carriage driver, I'd have laughed myself right off the fucking thing.

While we're on the subject of scrotums, you know what would be really uncomfortable? A wooden jock strap. Sure you would get plenty of support and protection, but I can't imagine it would be worth it for all of the splinters you would have to constantly be pulling out of your balls. I suppose that's why they use plastic.

SPACE, THE FINAL STRAW

I don't consider myself to be another Ralph Nader or anything, but every once in a while I like to come out with helpful suggestions for the hard-working consumer. With the state of our economy as it is, consumers have to look for any advantage they can find. That's why I want to present my own helpful tip. Just taking the opportunity to do my part.

Whenever you're making a purchase, and you feel that the price they're asking is higher than the item is worth, steal it. Just take the goddamn thing and walk right out the fucking door. What got me thinking about this was a Linkin Park CD that came out a few years back called "Minutes to Midnight". Before this CD, I loved listening to Linkin Park. The music was rich, yet hard and gritty. Exactly my genre of choice. However, something that they have always been guilty of is short-changing the customer when it came to the amount of music on a given disc. Since they have been with a major music label, they have, on average, put around 40 minutes of music on each CD. For a while, I was okay with this. A little uneasy, but generally accepting. Just about every song on the disc was good, or at least enjoyable enough so that I would be happy to listen to it multiple times. This latest disc that had come out was about the same in terms of music quantity; about 40 minutes. However, they must have dropped their quality standard right though the fucking floor, because it seemed that they put any old turd of a song on this album. At least half of the songs were complete and total shit. And they still had the nerve to charge full price for the fucking CD!

So next time you're at the music store, grab a copy of "Minutes to Midnight" and walk right out the door. Don't bother trying to hide it. Don't run. Just walk out. The alarms will go off. Fuck them. Keep on walking. And if someone comes chasing after you or calls the cops, you can tell them the truth. Tell them the CD is not worth the money they're asking for it, and to make up for all of the people that were duped into paying full price, you're taking the disc to balance things out. Be sure to tell them that you're performing a public service as well, since you're saving some other customer who might have purchased that very disc at a later date from getting ripped off and suffering disappointment. As the cop is dragging you off, reason with him. Make it clear that you and he are both the same; you're both protecting the public!

That whole deal with putting 40 or 45 minutes on a CD is bullshit regardless. The standard 700 MB writable CD holds 80 minutes of music. If you want to be generous, you can give them the benefit of the doubt and say they're using the lesser 650 MB, 74 minute CDs. If you have a band and you release a CD with only 40 minutes of music on it, you're wasting 34 minutes of recording space. That right there is a total rip-off! You wouldn't put up with that any other time you were buying something, would you? If you paid full price for a cell phone, and when you got it out of the box you realized it was missing the 1, the 4, the 6, and the # keys, you'd blow a fucking fuse! You'd go back to the dealer and say, "What is this shit?!? Gimme my fucking money back or I'll kill your family"!! Well, maybe you wouldn't use those exact words, but you would still be pissed. Or say you bought a case of beer, and when you opened it when you got home you realized 11 of the cans were actually Diet Fresca, you'd be ready to drive a tank though the beer store!

So if you buy a CD that doesn't have at least a solid 60 minutes of music on it, copy the disc or MP3 it, then take the disc back to the store and demand your money back. And if the clerk gives you a problem and starts spouting off about a no-return policy on open merchandise, them him "Fuck that"! You either get your money back or you're taking a shit in the cash register.

But also keep in mind that CDs aren't the only things that need to be stolen. Any type of merchandise should be subject to the principle. Even food! Some of you reading this had to have dealt with this at one time or another. You go to one of these fancy restaurants. You know, the ones who like to simulate night blindness when you come in from outside during daylight hours. And you have to wait a minute and a half before you can even see the fucking maître d'. And when you finally get to the table, the chairs look like they were constructed for an anorexic gymnast. The kind of chair that when you sit on it, you have to keep you butt cheeks clenched or you risk the chair going right up your asshole. You open the menu and you look at the prices. $20 for spaghetti. That shit costs 18 cents in the grocery store! And these fuckers are charging you an 11 thousand percent mark up for boiling it and throwing it on a plate. A steak: $45! But you figure "Fuck it. I'm here. I'm hungry. If I try to go outside now, my retinas are going to burn up". So you order something.

After waiting an hour and a half, because apparently they have a slaughterhouse in the back and they have to make a fresh kill for every customer, they bring out what appears to be a porcelain hubcap. This huge plate is almost the size of the fucking table! In the middle of it is this little stain of food, which they call an entrée. But unlike the aforementioned CD, they didn't waste the space on the rest of the plate, because they sprinkled the rest of it with about a pound and a half of dried parsley. Enough parsley that you ask to look at the menu again to see if that's what you ordered. But you keep your cool. You don't whip out your cock and start dick-slapping the waitress. You sit there civilly and you eat it. Naturally, it doesn't take long. It's 3 ounces of food. That's a 'bite' to me. You finish your wine, stand up and walk right out the fucking door. Don't even wait for the check. Don't even leave a tip. Just get up, walk out the door, get in your car, and leave.

Fuck those high-society ball lickers! Fuck them in the ass with a cattle prod! When they give you what you ordered, a $45 dollar steak, a steak that weighs more than the waitress, **then** you'll pay for it. Until then, fuck them. And if someone comes out chasing after you, turn the car around and run the cocksucker over! That's what he gets for charging $45 for a fucking steak. Caveat emptor? Let the BUYER beware? Bullshit, Jackson! Not in my fucking neighborhood!

30 SECONDS OF SHIT

If you're getting the idea that the majority of this book is aimed at bashing on commercial, you're wrong. It's no more than 50%, tops. Actually very little of this book is advertisement bashing, but I do have a few more that I need to get out before I'm completely done with the topic.

You may have to think back a ways, but there was this collection of Suave commercials. You may remember that they used opera music as a background. That was bad enough. For other people. I actually like opera, but that's a personal thing. Anyway, one of them involved what I kind of think of as the in-life evolution of a woman. It starts out with a young-looking woman getting engaged. It quickly shows her wedding, and then it moves right on to having kids. And she has one. Then another. Then another. Then...well, you get the idea. Her looks are degrading with every little crotch dropping that comes out of her. And then, she uses Suave. And just like magic, she's totally rejuvenated!

Let me tell you something you already know, though the industry has tried to convince you otherwise. I don't give a fuck what they put in shampoo nowadays. It isn't going to change the fact that you're now nailed down with a bunch of little misbehaving bastards because you can't figure out how to put your diaphragm in right. Nor does it have any chance of repairing your floppy, stretched-out, weather-beaten twat! In fact, maybe that should have been their slogan. Suave - Great for your hair, but it won't do a fucking thing for your busted pussy!

Speaking of vaginas, that leads me to another commercial gripe. Well, I can't say that my bitch is about the commercial. It's more about the product itself. It's called RepHresh (actually spelled that way in an attempt by their marketing department to be clever). The principle behind the product is that women use this gel or whatever it is (I've never had a need to use it myself) to take care of smelly vagina, or as I like to call it "Vaganus Syndrome", named after the phenomenon of a woman's snatch smelling like her asshole. The commercial says "After your period, RepHresh. After intercourse, RepHresh. After douching, RepHresh".

Now the first two seem logical. After your period? Definitely a good idea. Last thing a guy wants when he goes down on a chick is a surprise. No man wants to come up with a "raisin" on his nose. So the first one is good. After intercourse is also a good plan. The last thing a woman wants is a load of salty dick-snot fermenting in there for god knows how long. But then we come to the third one: after douching. Now, I may not be the sharpest cheddar in the dairy case, but I'm pretty sure of this. If you douche, and your pussy still smells like a spawning pool at Sea World, it's simply time to sew that thing shut! If Massengil doesn't keep you from lifting the lacquer from the floor you're standing over top of, fuck it! Close up shop! Someone is liable the get hurt.

Another commercial you may recall from a little while back was for Capital One home loans. It isn't the acting or the writing that pissed me off so much as the metaphor. George Carlin pointed this out in one of his books as well. Here's the scene: Some broad goes and gets a home loan with a variable interest rate. She's blond, so the set up so far is pretty realistic. Ha-ha! Oh, come on, girls. I'm kidding. You know I love you. How could I not?? Your throats go deeper than any brunette's...oh, wait. I seem to be losing track of the topic. It would seem my train of thought has taken a dirt road. As I was saying, she gets a home loan and from that moment on, a monkey appears on her back. And the filthy little, shit-slinging primate is breaking dishes, throwing paper everywhere, messing up her hair, everything!

Now let's first of all point out that the monkey on her back is a false metaphor. The monkey on one's back is meant to represent a harmful addiction, like smoking, drinking or shopping to name a few. In fact just about any word that can have an organization named for it ending in "Anonymous" is a prime candidate for the monkey metaphor. What the fuck does having a variable rate loan have to do with this?? Is she addicted to variable rate loans? Does she go from bank to bank getting these loans? Does she take the receipts for the closing costs and rub them into her crotch while moaning loudly? If she did, they didn't show it. Yes, that disappoints me. Regardless, it's nothing that can be called an addiction. Smoking, yes. Easily. Cheesecake, indeed! I have a little of that addiction myself.

Hell, even jacking off while listening to The Awful Show while a lesbian construction worker slaps you in the ass with used Dr. Scholl's athletic shoe inserts while singing various national anthems can be an addiction. Can't say I know anyone with that one. But, getting a variable rate home loan is not an addiction. It's just stupidity. Stupidity that commonly is copious in the jackoffs who write these fucking commercials. Maybe one of these days a few of these morons will learn to read a book not written by Dr. Seuss.

One commercial that actually reminded me of something that bothered me was one for DirectTV. They had a collection of commercials where they show what appears to be a scene from a movie or TV show and then one of the actors breaks off from the original script to go into a pitch. The one that was disturbing to me was the one with Pamela Anderson in Baywatch. If you didn't know, I'm normally all over anything dealing with spandex or swimsuits, but there's nothing even remotely appealing about that revolting panty stain. In fact, I can safely expand that to include anything that has been on the receiving end of a Tommy Lee ejaculation. Funny thing about that beach after the commercial was shot: It had an overwhelming smell of rancid fish. And it had nothing to do with the aquatic life.

Next example of half a minute in smart person's hell: Arbor Mist. I'm a wine guy. I don't drink beer. In fact I don't drink any alcoholic beverage that doesn't have a sweet taste, either naturally or being mixed with something. And Arbor Mist is just a tad drier than that Jewish wine, so technically I should like it, but after seeing this one commercial, it leaves a bad taste in my mouth. There's this backyard party; burgers and dogs on the grill, looks like a good time. Someone announces "Hey, Arbor Mist"! This one dopey broad perks up like Michael Jackson when someone says *little naked boy* (and yes, I know he's dead. It doesn't make it any less fun to bash on him though). The chick starts jumping across patio furniture, grabs a towel and start riding down a string of porch lanterns like she's fucking Indiana Jones, and lands right next to the drink cart so she can be the first in line. Everyone looks at her like she's got a penis for a nose, to which she replies, "Well, it *is* delicious". If I was the party host, you can be damn sure I would be saying something. *So, it's delicious, huh? That's why you had to wreck all my shit, you stupid cunt?? I don't give a fuck how delicious it is! Next time, your ass is walking around the patio to get a glass like everyone else, you fucking alcoholic twat!*

That leads us to another short-lived commercial that some of you may remember: Blockbuster vs. Netflix. Some chick and some black guy go out to get their mail. One has movies from Netflix, the other Blockbuster. And along comes this obese, unbathed, quadruple-chinned anal wart, and he's going to take it upon himself to tell them how their movies end. And then the one with Blockbuster goes off and takes the movies in to exchange them at a local store. Naturally the Netflix user is shit out of luck. First of all, this commercial is completely unrealistic. Perhaps you can call it taking artistic license or whatever, but here's a little more reality-based version of that same commercial. At least my reality.

The same chick and guy go to get their mail. One still has Blockbuster and the other has Netflix. The same fat ass-biscuit waddles along and spoils the movies for them. Here's where it changes. Instead of standing there dumbfounded, the two of them proceed to kick the shit out of this 5XL ball licker! The black guy pounds him with lefts and rights. The chick kicks him right in the fucking nuts, watches him crumple to the ground, then they both keep kicking him for 5 or 6 minutes. Call it an extended commercial if you will. And they leave him a bloody, whimpering pile of hemoglobin-soaked flesh and fat in the middle of the street. Then the one who uses Blockbuster has an epiphany, and sends the movies right back at the mailbox, goes into their place, gets on the computer and signs up for a Netflix account. And to close you hear "Netflix..." and whatever the hell their slogan is at the time.

Now, some of you may be wondering what the epiphany was. Well, I'll tell you. You see the problem with the commercial was trying to promote the idea of going into the store to exchange the movies. In order to take advantage of that notion, you need to interface with actual Blockbuster employees! Understand? You have to go into the fucking store and deal with some wretched, holier-than-thou pubic louse in a blue shirt and khaki pants earning $6.50 an hour. The same fucking skid mark you tried to avoid by getting DVDs-by-mail in the **first** fucking place. They should change the name of that place from Blockbuster to Cocksucker, because that just about describes everyone who works there.

One commercial that got me a little frisky once was Os-Cal. It's a calcium supplement for women. The one line was "Hips. You love them. You hate them. But you've got to protect them". For my money, hips are okay but what I really like is what's between hips: ass and vagina!! Unfortunately there aren't too many commercial for Ass and Vagina mineral supplements. At least not in this country.

This is a quick one. Pepsi has been through a lot of slogans over the years, but there was one I think they should have passed on. The slogan was "More Happy". Apparently they weren't seeing enough sales in the undereducated clientele. "More Happy"...It's HAPPIER, fuckheads!! Learn your fucking comparatives and superlatives, you stupid cocks!

There are some commercials that say things that go beyond the normal bounds of ridiculousness. Akavar was this weight-loss product a while back that claimed you could eat all you want and still lose weight. That was a pretty blatant lie, but the most hilarious part of the commercial came when they said "We couldn't say it on TV if it wasn't true". When the hell did that shit start?? Everyone on TV tells the truth all the time?? What a fucking load! If the FCC ever put that philosophy into use, there wouldn't be anything to watch on TV except PBS and the Discovery Channel. And even the latter is iffy.

Here's another product line I can do without. They have these undergarments called GoodNites. I think Luvs or Hugs or one of those diaper companies makes them. They are essentially diapers for older kids. Honestly, it doesn't matter what the commercial was or when it was made. As long as they advertise these things, they're going to be making light of them and that pisses me off, no pun intended. You'll hear them referred to a 'night pants' in some cases. Face facts; they're fucking diapers! I remember one commercial that had this little tard talking to the camera saying, "When I stay over a friend's house and I wet the bed, they laugh at me". No shit, Sherlock! You're 8 years old and you're still pissing your fucking pants! Of course they're going to laugh at you! I'm laughing at you right now, you pants-pisser!! You know something? You shouldn't even have friends! Learn to hold your piss without having to wear diapers, **then** go out and make friends, you disgusting little shit!

God damn it, I hate kids in commercials! Why do people need to parade their grotesque genetic abominations on TV? I think the Rice Krispies commercials are the biggest felons when it comes to this. One commercial has this little blond girl in it. This is one I can't watch without cringing. She's digging into the cereal with her bare hands. She put a strawberry on top of a spoonful with her hands and feeds it to her mother. And I'm going *Ewwww! That's disgusting!* Why would an intelligent grown person put anything in their mouth that children have touched? Little kids hands are nothing more than breeding real estate for disease. These little bastards don't get the concept that it isn't a good idea to play with the pile of dog shit outside, then pick your nose, then handle food. Now here's mom who just let Sally Germfingers shovel about 30 different kinds of pathogenic bacteria into her mouth, and 2 days later she'll be laying in bed with a 103-degree temperature wondering how it happened. Any adult who lets any part of a child near their mouth is just inviting infection.

Then they have another commercial with yet another little blond kid (Nazi Germany must have been running a special on child actors), and the kid is sitting there the whole time, babbling senselessly. *Bah bah blah blah bah blah blah bah bab blah blah!* And I'm yelling at the fucking TV after what seems like about 20 minutes of this shit. Shut up! Shut the fuck up, you little Hitler child bastard! And I'm picturing myself just thrashing the little fuck with a 2x4 until he's quiet. Or dead, whichever. I'm not picky. I either want intelligent conversation or quiet. There are your two choices. If the little shit isn't capable of giving me either of those, I'm perfectly willing to take any means necessary to mould the situation to meet one of those two conditions.

And people don't think I should have been a child therapist.

OPEN HERE, IF YOU CAN

I need someone to explain this to me. Pepsi has a 24-can packaging method called "The Cube". It's an arrangement of 24 cans in a 2x3x4 configuration that forms a cube shape, as if that weren't implied by the name. Duh. On the side of the box, it says "Easy To Open" and it has this sort of pseudo-perforation with the verbiage "To Open, Lift Up Here". Have you ever been able to open one of these fucking boxes the way it says you're supposed to?? I follow the instructions, and every time without fail, the glue on the flap lets go and it tears right up to the handle. And the tear is nowhere near the perforation! And now that the thing is torn, the handle is completely fucking useless. If you want to carry the thing, you need to pick it up from the bottom. And even then the cans have no sort of support and they fall out and roll everywhere. Grandma comes in from the other room, steps on a can, falls and breaks a hip. Thanks a lot, you Pepsi cumfarts! Nana's in the hospital because you brain-dead fucks couldn't even make a box right!

Apparently these cretins think that by simply drawing a dotted line on the cardboard and adding a shallow squiggly indentation along the line, the box will magically tear specifically on the line and nowhere else. Does it work that way? Fuck no! You don't need a degree in physics to know that the only reliable way to weaken the cardboard along the line is to puncture it all the way through in tiny increments throughout the line. I've looked at the other side of that cardboard too. I've held it up to the sun and examined it closely, which is probably a good indication of the amount of free time I have. But, there isn't a single photon of light coming through anywhere along that line. Next time any of you pick up a case of Pepsi, try your hardest to tear the cardboard along that line. Keep tearing until the cardboard gives along that line. I'll bet you that you'll end up with a pile of cardboard confetti before you can get it to tear along that line anywhere.

You know what these false tear lines remind me of? Those molded Styrofoam take-out containers. When was the last time you got take out and didn't have to deal with this shit: You take the box out of the bag, stick it in the microwave for a few seconds to warm the food up, open the lid and try to tear the top off so you can use the bottom part as a dish and not have to dirty up your own plates? Have you ever been able to get that Styrofoam to tear along that seam?? No! And you know why? Because the grain of the Styrofoam is always in the opposite direction! Why do the companies who make that shit do that?!? Are they intentionally trying to frustrate us?? You practically have to pull out a straight razor to get that lid off in a tidy manner. It's even tricky to do with a steak knife! And here's my theory, which also carries back to the Pepsi box dilemma. I think that when the machines making these lines compress the material, it's actually making it stronger in that area. If anything, the trick may be to start making the tear-away lines on the boxes by compressing the area AROUND the dotted line rather than right over it. Don't hold your breath for that to happen any time soon though. You know why? Because it makes sense!!

USER-FRIENDLY, MY ASS!

Here's a major bitch I have that as yet I've not gotten around to expressing. Computers. Not in general. Computers in general are great. If someone took away the Internet completely one day, I would lose my fucking mind. No, this is a very specific brand of computer. I've tried them all, too. From IBM originals, HPs, Packard-Hell, and even some bargain basement brands like Medion (Yes, I once bought a computer from a discount grocery store. Strangely enough, that thing lasted me over a decade)! However, never in my life have I used a computer so shitty, so utterly fucking worthless as a Gateway. If I took an empty mini-tower, took a huge shit in it (the kind you get after eating nothing but Mexican food and cheap beer for a week), stuck wires into it, put the cover on the box and plugged it into the wall, I'm positive I would be able to get more done using it rather than using a fucking Gateway! In fact, I'm pretty sure that's why every Gateway box has those black and white spots like a cow. Because, what's inside of a cow? Right, cow shit!! And that's precisely what Gateway computers are: a big steaming cow pie in a metal case.

It had been a long time since I had used a Gateway. When my old computer at work started to show it's age, I got to pick out a new one. So I'm looking through the ads and getting an idea of what's available and what I can get without breaking the bank. I saw some nice HPs, but I was kind of pissed at them about that time. I had recently had a need to buy new ink cartridges for an HP printer and if you have seen the prices on ink cartridges, you probably have a good idea of how bitterness can develop in a heartbeat for whatever make of printer you have. So that was out. Then I noticed there were several nice deals on eMachines computers at the time. They had some decent features and I'm all for giving a new manufacturer (or at least new to me) as shot. So I get one of those. First thing I notice when I take the thing out of the box is the shitload of stickers all over the front of the thing. Just about all manufacturers do that to flaunt what the computer has "under the hood". For myself, I don't like a lot of decorations on my computer, so I proceed to take the stickers off. Unlike other brands whose stickers easy to peel off without leaving residue, these are the kind of stickers you would put on someone's windshield to get revenge on them! The kind of stickers that take a half hour to get off, and even when you do, all the sticky stuff is left on it. And unless you have a quart of kerosene and a rag handy, that shit is there for good. The only other option is to take a bunch of Post-It notes and cover it up.

The first time I started it up, it was fine though. I got about 3 months out of it before the problems started surfacing. The first incident was that it started making a horrendous rattle any time you started it. In one day, my computer went from running relatively quiet to sounding like a fucking 1974 Pinto. So I do what any normal person does to make the rattle stop. I smack the side of it. True to form in the world of man-repairs, this stops the rattle. For about 5 minutes, then it was right back. Eventually it got to the point that I needed to take the bastard apart to see where the noise was coming from. It turns out the fan wasn't fitted right for that particular computer. Every time the fan would run, the rattle would come back. I tried tightening the screws. That didn't help. The only thing I could do to fix it was to bend the metal in such away that it would hold the fan in place better than it was.

Another couple months go by and I'm beginning to notice that ANY time you have more than 2 programs running, the auxiliary cooling comes on. And much like the former cooling apparatus, this motherfucker is **not quiet**! It sounded like there was a little maid inside the computer with a fucking vacuum cleaner. My patience for eMachines is coming to an end very quickly. The only thing I can do this time is take the side off the computer so the piece of shit will stay reasonably cool, and even that didn't help half the time. So here I am not a half of a year after my old computer was retired. I have a PC with synthetic snot all over the front of it, with no side on it and making more fucking noise than a airport terminal during spring break.

I consider myself a pretty sharp guy when it comes to technology, and to this day I can't figure out how it slipped past me for so long. I needed to go to the website to find out how to make a recovery disk. Just so I could try to start fresh, hoping against hope that I'll be able to squeeze another 3 months out of it. What do I find out incidentally? I discover that eMachines is the same fucking company as **Gateway**! It's the same motherfucking, cocksucking piece of syphilitic gorilla shit I tried to avoid in the first fucking place!!

Towards the end of the ordeal, I hoped and prayed that the electronic turd would overheat and catch fire. And you know what I would have done? I would have just sat back with a big smile on my face watching it burn. Just watch as the flames curled around and consumed that little fucking lowercase 'e'. I was half inclined to bring a bag of marshmallows into work just for the occasion. And get some graham crackers and chocolate too, so I could make s'mores. And it would have been just like a campfire. I would sit there singing Kum-Bay-Ya while the fire extinguishes came on and people were scrambling to get out of the building. But the funny thing about it. That computer would finally be capable of doing something productive...roasting marshmallows.

AND LINGO WAS ITS NAME, OH!

It probably goes without saying that I have little tolerance when it comes to watching commercial TV. But my scrutiny isn't just aimed at the commercials. I'm an equal-opportunity sociopath. I have just as little patience with the TV shows themselves. I recall watching an episode of Lingo on the Game Show Network that made me almost destroy my television.

For starters, the host, one Chuck Woolery (a well-known name if you have ever been a game show watcher), brings his worthless little vaginal turd of a son in front of the camera. And this is not a momentary appearance. He's on for the whole fucking show! I'm not big on the whole idea of people bringing their kids to work in the first place. It's taxing enough to have to see your face on a daily basis. What the fuck makes you think I want to see your repulsive, misbehaving offspring?? Keep the little bastards at home where they belong! Being on TV multiplies that whole feeling times a billion, though. As if this blatant display of nepotism weren't bad enough, he makes sure to explain the rules of the game to him at every turn.

Hey, Chuck! Some of us have been watching the show for three years now. We know how the shit is played. If Chuck Jr. needs a tutorial on the ins-and-outs of Lingo, then explain it to him on your own fucking time. As long as I'm watching the commercials, you can consider yourself on my clock, motherfucker! And I don't go for that shit! Put the little bed wetter in a day care and play the fucking game!

But the aggravation doesn't end at the Woolery family reunion. It just so happens that the contestants are geared to make me blow an aneurysm. The first one's name is Katie. At least it's spelled that way. But pretentiousness ever prevailing on GSN, she pronounces it 'Cot-ee'. *Hi! My name is Cot-ee! I'm an opera singer.* Fucking cunt! It's **Kay-Tee**! Learn the fucking rules of English and pronounce your name right, you pompous sauce-crotch rectal wart bitch!

Then it isn't insulting enough that a spotlight didn't fall from the rafters and crush her dead. But then her and her yeast-infection dyke of a partner go to the bonus round and win. And they didn't just win the standard $5,000. Fuck, no! As fate would have it, it had been quite some time since anyone had won the big jackpot, but sure as shit it would be won on this show! The fucking cum-catchers won $35,000!

Perhaps it's too much to hope for cosmic retribution on these clap traps just because they enraged me. But I can still hope for a day to come along wherein these two are walking down the street and some big, nasty, sweaty biker-type with bad teeth and the B.O. of a college basketball team grabs them up and ass-rapes the shit out of them until they vomit in terror. And they can't stop throwing up either! They just keep puking and puking until they fall down in a massive pool of their own stomach acid, sobbing uncontrollably until they die of dehydration. That would certainly teach those cunts to ruin my Monday night TV viewing!

NO SIR! THAT WASN'T MY FINGER!

I talk about driving a lot. Mostly because, with almost an hour and a half of commuting a day, it's just what I know best. But there are certain peculiarities when it comes to driving to work. I work for a large company. We have about 400 people working at my plant. As such I know a very small percentage of the people personally. Along with that, I know just as small a percentage of the automobiles the employees drive. I'm going on 13 years at the same work place so there are a lot of people above me and a lot of people below me. But I've noticed one thing: the closer I get to my place of employment, the less apt I am to flip off other drivers. And it's for one simple reason really: I don't want the other driver pulling into where I work right behind me and having it end up being some supervisor or something. The last thing I need is to get a termination notice with the space labeled "reason for termination" being filled with "flipped off the company president"!

And it isn't just superiors I'm concerned with. What if it turns out to be a customer? This goes for a lot of places that one can work. Can you imagine flipping some guy off at an intersection only to see them 3 minutes later asking them "Do you want fries with that?" It sure gives 'service with a smile' a whole new meaning.

But probably the biggest thing that bothers me about the rationing of finger gestures near my personal business place is the dishonesty of it. I pride myself on honesty and when I have to lighten up on bird-flipping simply in an effort to avoid professional conflict, I don't feel good about it. I think that more companies need to have rules of indemnity outside the workplace for personal interaction. If the president of the company is driving like a retarded little bitch, I need to have the freedom to put them in their place without fear of retribution when I punch the clock.

I guess the only other possible solution is eventually becoming my own boss. When you own your own company, that's when you know you have really made it. Not because you answer to no one but yourself, but simply because in traffic, you can let the bird fly with impunity!

JACK ME OFF

Jesus Cunting Christ! Yes, you read that correctly. This kind of shit pisses me off so much that I had to come up with a new compound obscenity. Before I go into this, please realize it's difficult to incorporate current news and events into a book. But this next subject matter should hold up despite the age of this book for the simple fact that even though the proper noun may change, there'll always be someone just like them around at any given time.

There's this little man-bitch by the name of Jack Thompson. He's an activist you may have heard of at one moment or another. I like to refer to him a Jackoff Thompson myself. And it's no shock that Thompson sounds a lot like Johnson, as in a dick. A floppy, lifeless, pimply, smegma-infested dick! For those who don't know this testicle-less fuck of which I speak, let me give you a crash course. Jackoff 101.

Jack Thompson is the piece of shit on the forefront of preventing the production and sales of violent or otherwise mature-themed video games. This zero-IQ, pinheaded prick is what I would call the head dean at the "violent video games are responsible for all the violence in the world" school of thought. In the simplest terms, he's just a total fucking retard!

One of his more notorious shooting-off-of-the-mouth incidents concerns a game I've gone on record in the past as praising. It wasn't the best selling game in the world, but that never changed my admiration of it. It's called Manhunt 2. Circa the release of the game, Sergeant Scrotum wrote a letter to the Florida Attorney General Bill McCollum and Florida Governor Charlie Crist. Here's an excerpt:

Florida retailers are scheduled to sell a very violent video game called Manhunt 2 *which will be available, remarkably, for "play" on the kids-friendly Nintendo Wii gaming platform.*

Did you notice that he actually put 'play' in quotes? What a fucking douche! I'll continue:

The Wii device does not utilize traditional push button game controllers but instead utilizes hand-held motion capture devices...It is a training device.

Hmmm. The Wii is a training device. Have you ever heard of anything so moronic in your life? Chances are if you're reading this, you have at least played Wii once or twice in your life. At any point did it feel like a replacement for, say, a

$200 million NASA flight simulator? Were you magically transported to the fantasy worlds of Zelda? Or perhaps you felt overwhelmed by the smell of beer and rental shoes when you played Wii Sports' Bowling! Perhaps, but chances are you felt like you were holding a fucking video game controller and playing a fucking video game!

I happen to be pretty good at Tiger Woods on the Wii. I'm speaking of his golf game, not a hooker simulator to clarify. By Jackoff's logic, I should be able to run right out and join the PGA. I mean they'd have to let me in. After all, I've received extensive training playing the game on the Wii! Funny thing though. When I go to the driving range, the furthest I've ever been able to hit the ball was about 150 yards, including the distance traveled with its near-boomerang slice! What's the deal, Thompson?? You said the Wii was a training device!

And what about Wii Sports? That comes with the system AND it's by Nintendo! That must be top-of-the-line training software there! I play all the games on there quite well, so not only should I be a pro golfer in the PGA. I should also be crushing home runs in the major league of baseball, I should be knocking out heavyweight champions in pro boxing, I should be bowling 300 games in the PBA, and I could be collecting grand slam trophies on the ATP world tour! Shit! I **have** to be able to do all that! I've been trained on the Wii! As yet, I haven't been successful in doing **any** of that!

Let's see what else this ass biscuit had to say. King Cornhole declared the game a public nuisance. I would love for him to clarify this. I've been stumped trying to make sense of it. Say you have one kid sitting at home playing one of the "worst of the worst", Grand Theft Auto. In that same area, across town, you have a kid who doesn't have a video game system. He's bored. He has no sort of outlet for energy, so he follows his friends who go out for a night of drinking. Needs to do something, right? There isn't shit on TV. He's already watched all his DVDs. He needs a new form of entertainment. They start hitting keggers at the local college. He pounds a few brewskies. Can't hurt, it's just beer. He mingles though the crowd and comes across a few guys toking up on a little weed. He's got a few drinks in him; he's feeling good. How about a little smoke? What's it going to hurt? Has some smoke and a little coke. Cocaine?? Absolutely! It's a party. It's all good! Snorts up a little nose candy. By this point he's feeling good! Really good!

His buddies say they're going to make a run to the mini-mart to get some snacks. Something to eat sure sounds good! That weed gave him a mean case of the munchies! So they run down there. Grab a couple bags of chips. Some Funions. Can't make a snack run and forget the Funions! Grab a big old Slurpie to wash it all down. It's just junk food. That never hurt anyone. He opens up his wallet. Oh, my. There's no money in there. Damn! What's he going to do now? Maybe he'll just wait until the clerk's back is turned and slip out. It's not like he's robbing the place! It's just a couple of bags of chips and a drink. Besides, don't these places have insurance for losses like that anyway? So he works his way to the door, waiting, waiting...and when the clerk turns his back to get a pack of smokes for someone, that's his chance. Everyone else is in the car ready to roll and out...he...goes. Oh, shit! The clerk turned back around and saw him. **Run!** If he can get to the car, he's home free. But, the car is pulling away. *Hey, get back here, you cocks!!* The mini-mart dude is still after him. Just as he thinks he might have a chance to get away, the beer starts working its way back up. Aww, man! He just threw up all over the place. That was a new shirt, too! If he wasn't so drunk, he might be able to run faster, but the clerk is gaining on him. And if he can't outrun the clerk, he may end up going to jail! He's got a nose full of coke; they'll throw the key away! Uh oh, the clerk caught him. It looks like he's going to have to fight for his freedom!

He throws a punch at the clerk and nails him in the face. The clerk throws a punch in return and nails him in temple. Ooh, that will make you see stars! He comes back and nails the clerk with a roundhouse kick, and the clerk hits the pavement. Wow, good thing he took those karate lessons instead of playing video games! That takes care of that, but the clerk saw his face. Oh wait, the clerk is trying to get back up! Fuck that! He lands another kick right to the ribs! Don't let him get up! Another shot to the ribs! Another kick to the spine! Boom, one to the back of the head for good measure. He's not getting up after that! He isn't even...moving. Look at all the blood. It's just pouring out of his mouth and nose. He...killed him. He hears sirens. It's the cops! The clerk must have hit the alarm before the chase, that son of a bitch! He'll have to try to out run the cops! On foot?? There's no way! He's out of breath and drunk. He falls to his knees. The cops jump out of the car and slap the cuffs on him, throw him in the back seat and haul him off to jail. And he's not getting out for a long time! Drug charges, burglary, resisting arrest, and the doozy, murder. And to top it all off, he's going to have one hell of a hangover.

But hey, at least he isn't doing something **really** harmful, like playing violent video games.

BARK(ER)ING UP THE WRONG TREE

It was sad for me when Bob Barker retired. Here I am, an avid fan of game shows, and one of the biggest, if not *the* biggest is losing its long time host. No one will be able to fill his shoes. I mean, he was the guy who kicked Happy Gilmore's ass. Fictionally, but still! So who replaced him?

Drew Carey. Drew fucking Carey. Here's a guy who has no talent to begin with. The unfunniest of 'comedians' second only to Jerry Seinfeld. And now his fat ass is going to be ushering up manic contestants for big cash and prizes. It's a crime. It really is. How many other highly notable game show hosts were around to choose from? At least a dozen! So what do they do? They pick a washed-up, loser comic.

I guess I should still be thankful they went with him. Do you recall who the other possible candidate was? I'll give you a hint. Big, fat, smelly dyke who wasn't even interesting enough to be on "The View". Give up? Fucking Rosie O'Donnell! That hippopotomine, toxic waste dump snatch of a muff diver! I can say without fear of contradiction that if she (and I use the term 'she' loosely) had gotten the job, "The Price is Right" would have been over, no more, kaput, done! When they held auditions for that show, thousands upon thousands of people would show up. They'd be lined up for blocks for the chance to get up on stage with Bob. Women of all ages wanted to kiss him on national television, and I'm sure a few guys did too! If Rosie took over, she would have been lucky to have even gotten enough interested people to keep contestants row filled for an entire show! I can see it now. Nine people in the audience. All the other seats empty. And when a contestant's name is called, they don't even bother running down. They stand up, let out a big sigh, and slowly make their way down to the stage. And when it comes time to bid, they don't even bother getting close, because they know if they do, they run the risk of having to go up that little half staircase...to her. A Hefty bag filled with cottage cheese wearing a pantsuit. The smell emanating from her crotch being enough to make your eyes water.

Next up for bids, this lovely china hutch! First guy bids. *Eight bucks!* Next bid. *Seven bucks!* Third bid. *Two million!* Uhhh, there aren't enough digits on the board for that. *Fuck it, I don't care, that's my bid!* Fourth bid. He doesn't even try to bid. He just starts sobbing uncontrollably and falls to the floor in the fetal position, sucking him thumb. And when she holds that big ham hock of a hand out to congratulate the poor fuck who won the bid, the contestant, with fear in their eyes runs off the stage screaming in sheer terror. Shit, the fat bitch could have just wiped her ass with that hand! I don't care if they're giving away 100 nymphomaniac female college gymnasts! It isn't worth the emotional scarring that will be sustained from having to touch that big, sweaty paw of hers. And if by some cruel twist of fate, Rosie had gotten the job, who were they going to get to yell "Come on down"? Ellen DeGeneres?? At that point they'd have had to change the name of the show to "The **Dyke** is Right"!

Fortunately, CBS chose the lesser of two evils. At least the contestants haven't throw up when they have stood next to Drew. Or at least they haven't shown it.

GSN, JUMPING THE SHARK SINCE 1994

Before I take leave of the game show topic for the time being, I have to try and see if I can stir up a few memories for my fellow game show junkies. Mind you it's a tiny memory as the two shows I'm going mention had the staying power of Crystal Pepsi, but I like to recall the ridiculous from time to time.

The first show was more of a tournament than a series. I guess if there was such a thing as a game show mini-series, it would qualify. It was called Grand Slam. The premise was pretty simple. Start out with a bunch of champions from other game shows and pit them all in an elimination tournament. A couple of the contestants happened to be John Carpenter (not the horror movie writer. He was the first millionaire on *Who Wants to be a...*) and Ken Jennings who won just a hair over $3 million on *Jeopardy*. That was the general genre of contestants; guys who had no chance of getting laid until the swarm of golddiggers moved in trying to cash in on their winnings. Sounds like fun, but alas, it suffered some fatal flaws.

There were some good matches in the early rounds, but problems arose when they hit the quarterfinals. In one match up, Carpenter has to go head-to-head with this sleazy little piece of trash named Michelle Kitt. She was apparently this female body builder who had been the big winner on *The*

Weakest Link a while back. I was looking at her and thinking if she was a bodybuilder, she wasn't very good at it. She must have been one of the puniest of all time.

Somehow she made it past the first round. She wasn't better than her competitor or anything, but here's how I think she advanced. The guy she went up against was a guy by the name of Kevin Olmstead. *Doctor* Kevin Olmstead, that is. This guy was a double whammy; he had won big on *Jeopardy* and *Millionaire*. If he was in fact a doctor, he must have been one of those ones who avoided the whole "practice what you preach" line of reason. He was a porker! When his round came up, it looked like wardrobe didn't have his size because he was about to burst out of his clothes. So he comes up against the steroid tramp, who is wearing this slinky little dress. Low neckline, high hemline, the works. I personally wouldn't have fucked her without a handsome financial reimbursement, but Olmstead must have seen something I didn't because he goes into this testosterone-induced panic. He was stuttering, hemming and hawing over every answer. Now, this guy isn't stupid! He made almost $2 and a quarter million off of trivia for fuck's sake! He knew the answers to the questions. The problem was that this manatee was constantly on the verge of blowing his load in his fucking pants! That would have fucked anyone up!

I was part of the Awful Show 3 on another game show called *Chain Reaction*, and I guarantee if the opposing team would have had 3 petite blonds in shiny metallic thong leotards, I wouldn't have given an answer the entire game! I would have just stood there with a lax jaw drooling all over myself for 30 minutes. Probably because I was too busy taking mental photographs to use later when I was rubbing one out! Shit, I would have probably rubbed out 4 or 5 in a row. I would have been shooting bone marrow after a while; I wouldn't have given a shit!

So, once she was done with fatty, she went up against Jennings, who I'm happy to say kept his dick out of the equation and handed Kitt her ass. Ass? Dick? Anal sex? What? Oh, sorry. Lost my train of thought for a second there once again. It happens more often with age.

Despite justice having been served in the end, the program had one other big problem: The hosts. The one host was Dennis Miller (who most people know as the funniest of Saturday Night Live "newscasters") and the other one was Amanda Byram (Ever heard of her? Don't feel bad. No one has. She was just another vacuous airhead slut anyway). I admit, I loved Dennis back in the days of SNL and I think his stand-up routines were hilarious. The problem with him being on the game show was he apparently thought the lines he used some 15 years ago were so funny that he'd just keep right on using them! In his defense though, if he were capable of writing new material, he would have never ended up across from some chair moistener in a red dress on a one-time game show. I guess we should have seen it coming. The movie "The Net"...what the fuck, Dennis?!? I know you're not smothered with job offers, but being a little selective from time to time wouldn't kill you!

The other show from our trip down memory lane was called "Without Prejudice". This wasn't even really a game show; I can't quite figure out how it found it's way on GSN. Maybe all the other stations turned it down. Process of elimination can play a big role in television production apparently. In this steaming pile of cowshit on video, there were 5 "contestants" and 5 panelists. One by one, the contestants are asked a variety of questions, and then they're kept or eliminated based on their answers. At the end, the last person standing gets $25,000. Big money for a GSN show actually. The biggest problem with this show was that instead of getting decent, respectable members of society for the panel, they seemed to be in search of the most repulsive gaggle of losers and jackoffs you would ever come across. I can only imagine them scouring bus stations and searching under overpasses for these retarded fucks. As if the show being on television wasn't enough of a crime against humanity (like that ever stopped *Survivor*), they had to pollute the commercial breaks with ads like "America's talking about *Without Prejudice*". I never heard anyone talk about the show, but if I had heard this omnipotent voice representing 'America', it would have probably been saying something like "Jesus Christ! Does this show suck"! I've wiped my ass and ended up with something more creative than this fucking turd of a program.

Let's just hope now that "America" never speaks of it again. Hmmm, now that I think of it, was the commercial referring to America Ferrera? That would make perfect sense because who would know better about quality TV programming than Ugly Betty. Mmmm, smell that? That's good old-fashioned home-cooked sarcasm there!

BIG RED BALLS GO PRO

The media has done all it can to take every imaginable sport and make a profession out of it. Football, basketball, baseball, hockey, soccer and even cricket! Well, not so much for that last one in the U.S. anyway. But it can't be far. It just needs one big sponsor to sign on and you'll end up with Friday Night Cricket. Sponsored by Krispy Krumpets or some shit.

There is, however, one sport that hasn't seen the likes of free agency and salary caps. Kickball! Remember that? It was just about the favorite sport in elementary school gym class! It didn't require the slightest bit of talent to play! They rolled that big, red ball, which for some reason had "GYM" written on it. As if there was some use for them in Social Studies. The ball got to you and then, **BOOM!** You kicked it! Sometimes it went way up high. Sometimes it rolled along the ground. And even, on occasion, it flew right out and nailed the pitcher in the groin! And then you ran the bases, which were about one quarter the distance of the ones in baseball. Even the physically disadvantaged had a chance for a 'base hit'.

But, as I was originally saying, it's one sport that has never gone pro. I don't see why not. I think it would be fucking great! The PKL - Professional Kickball League! Every major city would have a team. You take all the college soccer players and football kickers that weren't good enough for the pros. You'd have kickball arenas! A fraction of the size of regular stadiums, but with plenty of seating for noisy, drunken fans! And of course you would have the standardization of other sports. For instance, pitchers wouldn't have playground rules to follow. None of that granny pitch bullshit. They'd have training like those big, softball bull dykes that swing that huge arm around and fire the ball at you like it was shot out of a cannon. I'm waiting to see something like that. And you know it will happen too! So you'd better get in on the ground floor while the stock is affordable.

Kickball Fever! Kick it one time, home-booooyyyy!

A SALTIN' FOOLERY

Here's a fun joke to use on a salt junkie. I probably thought this one up based on the fact that I am one. We can smell our own kind.

Go up to them and ask them if they were stranded on a desert island (yeah, here we go with this shit again!) and they could have all the food they wanted, but were only allowed one seasoning, what would it be. Unless they're on the ball that day, they'll probably say 'salt'. Then you can laugh at them. Tease them about how they wouldn't need it because they'd be surrounded by salt water. All they'd have to do is evaporate it! Okay, maybe that is far from the funniest joke in the world, but what do you expect from a **clean** Keyz joke??

Don't tease them too hard about it though. You know those people and their blood pressure. You don't want to give them a fucking cardiac. Also, the perceived cleverness of this joke relies on the person's ability to disregard all of the fish piss and medical waste contamination.

THAT IS A HARDEE MEAL!

I frequent Hardee's whenever I get a chance. Some of you may be more familiar with Carl Jr.'s. Same place really. But I absolutely love eating from there. They know how to make a fucking burger! They're not like places that cook the shit out of the burger, so you're left with little more than a fucking patty of burnt beef jerky between 2 pieced of bread. No, the way they cook their burgers are the way you would do them on your grill at home. They're so juicy, just looking at one is enough to make your teeth ache thinking about that first bite. I bet I got your teeth aching right now just describing it! Hahaha! But seriously, **that** is a good burger!

The funny thing is they aren't satisfied with just giving you a great tasting burger. They have to try to feed you the most massive thing you can even try to fit in your mouth. Insert your own sexual comment here while I continue. They have what's called a 2/3-pound burger. That's 0.3 kilograms for all you Euro-fucks. But that's an amazing idea! I can only imagine the meeting at Hardee's headquarters when they came up with that idea!

Hey! Let's make a burger that not only will make the customer have to dislocate their jaw to eat it, but that's so big it just kills them! They'll take the last bite and their heart will explode!

Good call on that one guys. Way to maintain a clientele. But there was one other thing I noticed. They have double burgers. Well hell, every restaurant has double burgers. Even the fucking places that don't serve burgers, somehow 'double burger' found its way onto the menu. Some of those places even have them all way up to four burgers. The double-double! That's good for your cholesterol! Why don't you just jam one of those in my aorta? But no place that I've ever been to has a double chicken. Not one fucking place does that. How hard is it to get one enterprising burger joint to throw two chicken patties on a bun? I can do it myself, I guess. Next time I'm at a place, I can order two chicken sandwiches, then take the one patty and put it on the other sandwich, then throw the empty bun away. No, fuck that! Too much work. I didn't go there to engage in a sandwich reconstruction project. I came there to fucking eat!

I KILL ME!

Here's another one that's going to make all the moral-minded people shit an armadillo. I don't care, I'm writing it anyway. I do not understand why people feel suicide is such a deplorable act. I can understand that it's messy, sometimes more than others depending on the method used. But come on, there are people who get paid to clean that shit up. It's good for the economy!

But aside from the bounty of capitalistic benefits, I want to examine some of the other aspects of it. Suicide is unlike any other crime. Think about this: If you fail at it, you can be locked up, but if you succeed at it, there's no punishment. That's pretty fucked up! How can anyone take that seriously!

Can you imagine if that carried over to other crimes? If I rob a bank, but I make it to the getaway car before the cops show up, I get to keep the money and don't have to go to jail! I doubt the law is going to change to meet that scenario any time soon, but I'll keep my eye on the law books.

But let's look past the legal aspect and examine the religious viewpoint. Catholicism says that it's a moral sin. If you kill yourself, you go to hell. But think of how concerned with logic and reason the Catholics are. It would probably be just a little too much to ask they change that now. I think there's a better chance of seeing that bank-robbing law change first. So since I'm big on logic, let's go ahead and examine suicide from a logical viewpoint.

We'll start from an ecological perspective. By committing suicide, you're helping to contribute to the food chain. From all the treehuggers you've heard spouting off over the years, you must realize that Mother Nature needs our help. There you have it! By putting yourself to death, you're feeding mother earth and giving back after taking so much, which we all as humans are guilty of. So suicide is at least an environmentally sound decision. How can that be considered bad?

Now, we know that Earth Day only comes once a year, and if it was that fucking important, it would have gotten a whole month. So let's take a view from society. That seems to be much more in the spotlight when someone "takes the easy way out". At first glance, it may seem that suicide is an irresponsible decision. People will naturally be upset, there'll be a lot of broken-hearted folks, but the truth is that they'll get over it. You've heard the phrase "life goes on"? That isn't just some cold, heartless shit people say to you after you just got dumped. It applies to exactly this sort of thing! It will hurt for a while, then people will move on.

But when the term 'society' is used, it rarely refers to just a small group of people, like one person and their friends and family. It's usually considered to be more in terms of a nation of people. "American society" is a common phrase that demonstrates that semantic usage. So what's the societal take on suicide? I think there's not much of an argument against the idea that this planet is overrun with people. If you happen to be one of those people who don't agree with that (and you're a fucking idiot if you don't, by the way), think about being in rush hour traffic, when you can't look ahead of you or behind you without seeing a seemingly endless line of cars. Think about when you go to a concert or sporting event. Stadiums and ballparks used to be much smaller, and if you think that the reason stadiums are bigger now is because sports are more popular, you're full of shit. It's because there are **way** more people now! Still not convinced? Here's a clincher for you: Think about going shopping the day after Thanksgiving! Ahhh, I knew that would do it! That's for the women anyway. For the men, think about shopping the day before Christmas. That is, after all, our equivalent. When you're surrounded by people, so much so that you can't walk 50 feet without having to squeeze around or bump into someone, you're experiencing the early effect of overpopulation. And that's just in the United States! In other countries, it's far worse! The U.S. hasn't even come close to the full effect. Be sure to ask someone who has been to China or India about that. It's like the busiest shopping day at a mall, but it's **everywhere** and **all the time**! And the sad truth is that it keeps getting worse every single day.

In 1950, there were approximately 2½ billion people on the planet. At the time of this writing, mid-January of 2010 just 60 years later, it's estimated that there are just under 7 billion. That's almost triple! And in another 40 years, it's estimated that you can add 2 billion more to that.

When one makes a decision to end their own life, it's actually an (albeit unintentional) effort to lessen the strain on our already limited resources. This applies in 2 different respects. First, the person who is no longer alive is no longer using up food and clean water. They're no longer using gasoline. That's a big one since the world is quickly running out of fossil fuels. The only gas the deceased will be using will be for the hearse, but even that's a one-time trip. Every resource normally consumed by most every other human is no longer required for that person. Secondly, the ability of the person to produce offspring, making the population and global strain even higher, isn't an issue anymore. Either intentionally or unintentionally, procreation has ceased to be a concern for that individual.

With all these benefits to the earth and its people, suicide is a very socially responsible act. If you're disgusted by that summation, don't complain to me; complain to Mother Earth!

WHO ARE ADULTS KIDDING?

For those of you reading this who are minors (Shame on you! Hah! Not really,) there's no doubt that you have heard adults tell you about how great it is to be a kid. They've said things like "you should savor your time as a child" and that "these are the best years of your life". They have fed you the line that "being an adult is hard" and they "wish they could go back to childhood". One of the most popular phrases they'll use is "the real world", and that's not referring to an MTV series. I'll be 39 in June of this year, 2010. That qualifies me as being an adult by most standards, and I would like to take a moment to help clear up some things about adulthood.

Whenever you hear someone implying "being an adult is not all that it's cracked up to be", you can rest assured that they're totally full of shit! Being an adult is fucking great!! I'm not saying that it doesn't have its shortcomings. Paying bills can be a pain in the ass, and you have to work for your "allowance", but believe me when I say that's a very small price to pay (no pun intended)! When you're an adult, though, you can buy anything you can afford any time you want. You don't have to ask anyone's permission to do just about anything. If you want to stay out until 3 in the morning, do it! Drink your self silly. **Alcohol**! That's another big one! You can go into a liquor store (or grocery that sells booze for anyone outside the medieval laws of Pennsylvania), grab all the hooch you can carry, take it up to the counter and buy it, and the worst thing that will happen is they'll ask for ID. It's fucking awesome!

I don't want to totally discount one other downside to being an adult, however. It will no longer be legal to have sex with underage girls. That isn't to say that you can't get an eyeful of them at the mall, then go home and masturbate later. So it doesn't take that much away.

Just remember not to believe your parents when they feed you that shit about adult life being harder, because that's exactly what it is. Grade-A bullshit. Just like they lied to you about Santa Claus, the Easter Bunny, and the Tooth Fairy. The fact that you don't believe in them anymore doesn't change the fact that parents are the worst kind of liars. So the next time your parents feed you the line "just wait until you're an adult", tell them to blow it out their ass, and tell them Keyz sent you. And if they ground you for mouthing off to them, at least you can sit in your bedroom and imagine how great it will be when you become an adult. Sweet dreams, kids!

PATENT PENDING #1638492

I live in a small town that has a very irritating problem. The traffic lights. The timing of the traffic lights make it impossible to get from one end of town to the other without hitting at least 15 red lights. That may not sound like much but you have to keep in mind we only have 22 intersections! Anyway, they really got me in an uproar one week and, while I don't remember the exact rant, I do know that it ended in "...because the traffic lights are all pissfucked!"

Pissfucked. I've been notorious for concocting compound profanities, but for some reason, this one was especially thought-provoking. Here's my explanation of said adjective.

The term 'fucked' has long been used to describe an unfavorable state of being. As one can probably assume, 'fucked' is a shortening of the full phrase 'fucked in the ass'. While literally getting fucked, outside of a rape situation, is often quite pleasurable, getting fucked in the ass tends to be rather uncomfortable, especially when it's unwelcome. Now say that while you were getting anally penetrated, the intruder took it upon themselves to urinate into the body cavity. It would turn an uncomfortable situation into a more than likely messy and possibly biohazardous scenario.

Therefore, when something is really bad, worse than just being the garden variety form of 'fucked', it can be said that it is *pissfucked*. While this is my personal term, I'd like everyone to feel free to use it. Just remember where you heard it first and please use it properly. I hate when people use pissfucked grammar.

TOO MUCH OPTIMUS PRIME RIB

Since the recent rebirth of the Transformers, thanks to Michael Bay, I got to thinking about them. I was a fan of Transformers from back in the 80s. This was before all those 3-D modeling, ultra-realistic effects. Back then we were lucky to have Claymation for that shit. This was old school Transformers.

But here in an age of political correctness and universal sensitivity, I have to wonder...Why are there no fat Transformers? I'm not talking about the ones that are short and stout. They have plenty of them. I'm talking about ones that, were they made of flesh, would be considered clinically obese. And yes, I know machines don't get fat. They don't require food or anything like that, but you could still make some connections. Like say one didn't get his oil changed enough and now he's worse for the wear. He can't keep up with the others when they charge into battle. They can't transformer without having to stop halfway and catch their breath. I think it would be kind of refreshing to see something like that. You could even use it as a cautionary tale. One Autobot didn't get his air filter changed last time he was in the shop, he gets winded and Megatron comes out of nowhere and blows him into fucking oblivion. Then, like G.I. Joe, they tell you too eat right and exercise or some shit. Because knowing is half the battle. Even if you're a car that turns into a CD player.

FOR BETTER OR WORSE

Marriage is love under contract. This is not malice or spite or anything like that. True, I've been divorced twice, but that has nothing to do with that notion. I enjoyed being married when I was, but without mincing words, in black and white that's exactly what it is.

This leads me to believe that weddings could be a lot different, both in execution as well as outcome, if we treated the vows as an approach to a legal unification like any other. I can just imagine how many more "I don't"s you would get if you referred to the husband as the party of the first part and the wife as the party of the second part. I mean, fuck, that's how they're referred to whenever the divorce rolls around! Shouldn't something like that be standard across the board? I don't think it should be so hard to come up with a little consistency once in a while.

SOCIETAL CLEANSING

When it comes to finding the lowest rung on the ladder of society, you don't have to look much further than your local Laundromat. Or launderette for those of you reading this across the pond. My apartment building has its own washers and dryers so I'm pretty well set, but one time a roommate talked me into going there. They said it would be easier or quicker or some shit. I don't remember; I think I was still a little drunk from the night before. Regardless, this experience left me with a little more knowledge of society as a whole. For instance, I now know that if at any given time you're in search of the crème de la crème of human repulsion, you'll find it at a Laundromat.

When I was there, I tried to use the change machine to change a $20 bill, which surprisingly that machine accepted. If you have never had the chance, I'll be the first to tell you it's a lot of fun! It's being in Vegas without any chance of losing the house payment. You stick the $20 in and it spits the quarters out one at a time. Cha-ching, cha-ching, cha-ching, cha-ching, cha-ching, cha-ching, cha-ching, for like 5 fucking minutes! It's great! However, on this particular visit, the change machine was not working. So I voyaged to a handful of local businesses to try to accumulate enough quarters to do at least the important laundry. I was able to shmooze about $9 worth, which was plenty. I load my clothes in the machines, dump in some detergent, stick the quarters in and get them running. I'm all set so I have a seat.

And then, here they come.

The first guy through the door is this real piece of used toilet paper. Big dumpy fuck with a tank top on. Yeah, that's exactly what my venture to the laundry needed; the stench of some guy's armpit unabated filling the room for the next hour and a half. He's got cut-off shorts, white tube socks and hiking boots on. This guy looks like "The Thing That Came From Walmart"! It took every bit of control I had to keep from falling on the ground laughing at this fuck. So he goes to use the machine. Like the nice guy that I am...well, not really, but like the nice guy someone else might be, I tell him that it's broken. He asks, "What did you do?" which in his particular dialect sounded more like "Joo doo?" I wasn't sure if he was talking about some form of martial arts or if he was referring to a Hebrew's haircut. So I take a peek in my Redneck-to-English phrase book to figure out what he just said, and after translation told him I went around to a few neighboring businesses. I also told him that Pizza Hut told me Marathon (the next door gas station) had a change machine. He spouts out something like "Marathon ain't got no change machine"! So I go ahead and reply, in his dialect so he'll understand, "Well, I guess yoos just shit outta luck then, ain't cha??" Fucking asshole. That's the last time I try to help his hillbilly ass out. *How about I take that high-quality bottle of generic detergent you brought and shove it up your fucking ass, you fucking hard-on!*

And then as if that wasn't bad enough, the next one had to be something right out of the movie "Wrong Turn". This son of a bitch makes Garth Brooks look like Luciano Pavarotti. At this point, my stuff is in the dryer and I know I'll be gone soon, but this guy is bent on bringing true meaning to the phrase 'painful to the very end'. So this schmuck heads over to the manager and goes "that machine ain't workin' and I already gots my clothes in it". And I'm muttering to myself, teeth gnashing, saying "then I guess yoll just haffa take 'em out and put 'em in a different one 'nere, hayseed"! Or maybe that was too complicated for him. Christ! This is the type of dumbfuck who stops at a stop sign and waits for it to change before he goes. Much like his gene pool's evolution, not going anywhere!

It was a learning experience though. I learned that if I ever have to go to the Laundromat again, I'm washing my fucking clothes by hand in the bathtub!

Before I depart from the laundry discussion, I want to pose a question. When you go to buy a laundry basket, do you even show an interest in buying a round one? Those things are fucking ridiculous! They may have seemed like a good idea to someone at one time, but after using one you have to realize how inconvenient they are. First off all when you carry them, they either bend inward (which will split the rim of it in a heartbeat. You ever get you hand pinched in the crevice of a split laundry basket rim??) or they make a big concave dent in *your* side. And then whenever you go to put your clothes in them, you either have to dump them all in and fold them when you get home or you put them in and have all the corners of them fold upward! The only other option is to somehow fold them circular, but who the fuck can do that? It's like year 2 Calculus. Fuck it; I'll just buy the square one like an intelligent person. Save those round baskets for tomatoes or cantaloupes. At least that shit is round.

DIET IS 'DIE' WITH A 'T'

There is this alleged miracle weight loss product that's moderately recent and goes by the name "Alli". It's some pills that come with a little blue case. Either that or it's just this blue thing you stick in your mouth to keep you from putting food in it. I'm not sure. I think it's a pill case, though.

Anyway, while you're taking the pills, here are the rules. #1 - you need to change your diet. #2 - you have to exercise more than you have been. #3 - don't expect immediate changes. #4 - it won't work if you don't have the discipline to stick with it. Okay, so tell me: Where's the big fucking miracle. First off, if I had the discipline, and if I exercised, and if I controlled my eating, and if I had even a little bit of patience, I wouldn't be the big fat fuck I am in the first fucking place! Tell you what, assholes! When you geniuses invent a product that's indisputably and clinically proven to burn off 20 pounds of fat with one pill while I sleep, then be sure and let me know. I'll rush right out and get it. Until then, don't hand me a bottle of placebos with a little case and tell me that in order for it to work I have to do everything that would make me lose weight anyhow. There's a term for that shit you're selling: snake oil!

PEGGY PHELGM-ING

Did you ever have a ball of snot in the back of your nasal passage? And you try to blow it out and it just won't go? So you have to try to suck it back so you can spit it out? And when you do, the thing hits the back your throat at about 100 miles per hour? Then you sit there coughing for about 10 minutes and people keep asking if you're okay? Doesn't that really suck? And did you notice I just asked 6 questions in a row and this is actually number 7?

Okay, I'll stop that now.

4 WHEELS DOES NOT A CAR MAKE

Here's a little advice for the automotive niche. You guys who are gearheads and such. Just because your car is older than most of the ones on the road doesn't mean that you have a 'classic' car. Age alone does not merit that distinction. Pay close attention the next time a car show comes to your town and you'll see what I mean.

The 'classic' cars you see in a car show will have a certain look to them. You'll see lots of very old cars; some from the 60s and the 50s and maybe even some older than that. You'll see car models that were the peak of good taste back in their day. Models that perhaps only the societal cream of the crop might have owned. The cars themselves will be shiny and glistening with polish with light dancing off the flawless chrome. Cars that look like they just came off the showroom floor. That's what a classic car is.

Now have a look at your car. If it has "Classic" plates on it, it should match this description. When you're driving a 1970-something piece of shit VW beetle that has scuffed paint and bumpers rusting off the frame, you're not driving a classic car. You're driving something that, chances are, does not even belong on the fucking road. Here's an excellent point of reference. If your car is something that you might have driven when you were in college when you couldn't afford an actual car from a dealer, you're not driving a classic car. If that isn't clear enough, let me try putting it another way. If the vehicle in question is something you were driving when your diet consisted mainly of Raman noodles and Kraft macaroni and cheese, that car is probably not something that should be taken to a show and flaunted. If you're driving a vehicle like this and it has classic car plates, let's try and get in touch with reality. Take a screwdriver and remove the classic plates. Put the old plates back on, turning the screws gently. Otherwise the fucking bumper may fall off under the stress. Drive the car to the junkyard and trade it in for $80 scrap value, then go and try to get financed for a real fucking automobile. In the event you can't get financed for a real car, $80 should be able to get you a good 3 or 4 months worth of bus passes. Plenty of time to pedal your ass around town looking for a job that might make you finance-worthy or possibly even give you sufficient funds to purchase a real car.

I'm just trying to help.

GET YOUR RED-HOT ORANGE STYROFOAM HERE!

Every once in a while when I'm in the grocery store, I'll happen across those bags of circus peanuts. You know, not actual peanuts from the circus! I'm talking about those bright orange (or as I like to call them 'nuclear orange', because I'm pretty sure the fucking things glow in the dark) marshmallows that are in the shape of big peanuts. If you have never made physical contact with a bag, I want to make clear that these are not fresh marshmallows. They're *aged* marshmallows. Much like wine or cheese, there's apparently a waiting period from the time they're fresh to the time they're packaged and shipped. My only question about this is: Who the fuck still eats these things??

Don't get me wrong. I can understand the novelty of them when they first came into being. Back in 1892. But get real, it's over a century later and it's time to let them go to the retired candy hall-of-fame. Right along with those sugar dots stuck to a piece of paper and those wax bottles that have about a half drop of sugar goop inside.

It would seem apparent that some people are still eating these things. If you happen to be one of those people who never made the mistake of eating one of these, here's a description of what you're missing. These are one of the most nauseatingly sweet food items (term used loosely) that you can put in your mouth, next to cotton candy that is. Cotton candy will always be the king when it comes to sugar snacks. There was a great idea! Let's take sugar and spin it around really fast to give it the consistency of a spider web. Mmmm, delish! But other than this taste treat, you'll never find anything sweeter than circus peanuts. At least without a prescription. When you eat one of these, just one, your blood sugar will go up 90 points in 3 seconds. And if you're suicidal enough to attempt to eat an entire bag of these things, you'll become a diabetic. Instantly! Congratulations, dipshit! I hope you like pricking the end of your finger!

Seriously, I would think by now that if they still insisted on making circus peanuts, they'd at least have the courtesy to put a warning on the bag. *Warning: May cause glucose-induced coma. Do not consume while driving.* There are certain means of public safety that need to be utilized.

BLURB OF CONSCIOUSNESS

Doesn't the word 'blurb' sound like it should be short for something. It just doesn't seem like a complete word to me. Like when you pick up a book, like a hardback with a dust jacket, and you open it and look on the inside cover, there are a few paragraphs that summarize the general idea of the book. That's what they call a blurb. But it still seems like it used to be a longer word at some time. Like "blurbography". When someone writes a biography, it isn't uncommon for it to simply be referred to as a 'bio'. I think 'blurbography' is where 'blurb' came from. They both refer to a written work. Sounds logical to me.

Or maybe it was like the term 'burbs', that of course being short for 'suburbs'. Could it be that 'blurb' is short for 'sublurb'? That works too. Since 'sub' means "less than", a sublurb could be like "less than a book". Just a taste of a book.

That's one thing I could never quite figure out. Sub- is a pronoun meaning less than. And 'suburb' is short for 'suburban'. Now, the word 'suburban' would be broken down as 'less than urban'. But this doesn't make sense to me. When you see housing in an urban area, you rarely see any nice houses. Usually it's some shithole row homes with no garages, no backyards, nothing but a pile of bricks with some welfare leech living in it. Now picture a suburban home. Nice big yard, a garage, sometimes 2-car, nice trees and shrubs growing. A very pleasant scene. To me, the suburban house is a lot better than the shitty urban housing. So if anything, why shouldn't we call the nice house with the big yard "superurban" – bigger and better than the 'urban' home. Then if you need to shorten it, it would be 'superurb', though that's kind of difficult to say without it sounding like 'superb'. And while the houses are superb compared to the urban house, there is...the...umm...suburb...sublurb...dust jacket...

What was I talking about again?

PLAY THAT REDNECK MUSIC, WHITE BOY

I don't think there has ever been a stupider name for a music genre than 'country'. What country? Scotland? I've heard a lot of bagpipe music, but no one has ever referred to it as 'country'. Maybe it's the U.S., but that's a little fucking presumptuous! Is it the official music of the nation? I never authorized that. In fact I highly doubt you're even going to find **half** of the U.S. population listens to that hillbilly shit! That's like the Dallas Cowboys being called America's team. Fuck you! I hate the Cowboys. I'm an American and I couldn't care less if the entire team choked on a big Mexican dick! Country is just a stupid name for music from the start because it implies a region. When was the last time you heard of 'City music'? How about 'Borough music'? Town? State? Province? District? Not a one of those has its own music. But country does. Does it go by size? That can't be because there are plenty of countries that are smaller than some of our states. So, right off the bat, it's bullshit.

Now, what about the content. I've heard the lyrics to country songs. When they aren't about drinking beer to the point of brain damage or beating up queers, it's about how some woman broke their heart. I want to examine this a little further just to make sure I'm getting it all correct. Here's a cowboy, a tough hombre, a bad living-of-the-land motherfucker, a roughneck hard ass. A guy who uses hedge clippers to shave. A guy who drives a big ass pickup truck; a truck so big it blocks out the fucking sun. A guy who not only has a lump of tobacco the size of a baseball stuffed in his cheek, but the tobacco is liberally blended with horseshit just so he can prove to everyone he's tough enough to handle the taste. A real macho dude, and here he is before us crying about how some woman, the fairer sex, a dainty beautiful flower of the species, broke his heart. This 100% leather-skinned, Ford-driving douchebag just can't handle it when the woman that they have been beating the shit out of regularly for 2 years says she has finally had enough and walks out.

You know what I say? Suck it up, you shit-kicking pussy! You're suppose to be some kind of alpha male who gets tossed by a 2,000-pound bull, gets their leg ripped off, and reattaches it himself with a staple gun and duct tape because they're too tough for a hospital. And then you cry and you whine about how some woman left you. Go cry on your fucking chicken-fried steak and suck a dick, you phony shit-for-brains cocksucker! John Wayne is rolling over in his motherfucking grave having to listen to your pussy-ass shit! Jesus!

And take off that stupid fucking cowboy hat! What the fuck is this a Halloween party?!? Fucking retard!

DIDN'T I SEE THOSE IN A PORN SHOP?

I don't know if they still sell these, but you had to have seen them at least once or twice before they stopped trying to scam people. The popular brand name for these things was "Tater Mitts". I've never touched these things with my own hands, but from my personal observations, I can conclude that these are rubber gloves that someone took finely-ground asphalt and coated the palm surface with. What you're supposed to be able to do with these things is take a potato and, while running it under water, rub it and like magic the skin comes right off. If these wonder-gloves actually worked that might be mildly cool. I'm a modern man; I know my way around the kitchen. However, I'm a man, and I got to thinking that while using these in the kitchen would be okay, I think they'd be put to much better use if you kept them on your nightstand. If someone went to a warehouse where they keep all the unsold "as-seen-on-TV" stuff, bought up all the Tater Mitts and sold them to a porn shop for use in the masochist masturbation area, they could become a millionaire overnight. I'm not a virgin to the whole kink thing. I'll gladly tell you there are sick fucks like me out there that would love to get their hands on a pair of "Ground Beef Mittens"! Ain't nothing like a bad case of road rash on your pecker to liven things up in the bedroom!

THAT WAS MY PLAN ALL ALONG!

I don't want to keep bouncing back to commercial bashing but this is one that really made me think. Not about the product, but about the potential brilliance some of these ad executives may have after all. There was a commercial a few years back for CholestOff. I don't know if the company is even still in business or not, but I remember that name. And let me tell you why I remember it.

In their commercial, they had a guy (who they took great pains to let you know his name was Tom. No last name. Just Tom.) who was your average, garden-variety guy off the street. Completely unspectacular in every sense of the word. Tom (His name was Tom by the way. Just wanted to make sure you didn't forget, because it's *so* fucking important) apparently took CholestOff and had good results. While he was giving his opinion on this product, they superimposed a graphic of a portion of what he had said. Here's a guy with no sort of professional credentials or pedigree whatsoever, and they're doing graphical overlays of his words like he's some kind of fucking celebrity. Now, here's the best part. You want to know what his words of wisdom were? What lyrical phrase was so profound that they had to share it both audibly **and** visually?

I can't believe it. - Tom

Wow! That is something! Tom (Tom is his name for the record), some Joe Six-Pack from Gopher Sack Junction, Alabama, let his jaw drop and drool out the epic and philosophical phrase "I can't believe it". Well, holy motherfucking shit! Fuck me running with a frozen red snapper! I had just better run right out and pick up a whole case of this shit because Tom (That name again is Tom) said, and I quote, "I can't believe it"! I swear when I saw this I almost pissed my pants laughing. I went online and researched to see if it was an actual product because I would have sworn I'd stumbled onto an episode of Mad TV or something.

At first, that struck me as the stupidest, most vacuous, brain death inspiring commercial I had ever seen. At first. Because you see, the wisdom in this commercial ran far deeper than its kindergarten-esque façade. There were truly some great minds at work on this. I can picture it almost like I was there. A brightly lit room with plush leather chairs filled with ever-widening executive asses. The one at the head of the table rises, clears his throat, and then speaks...

Gentlemen, here's my proposal for our next commercial. Let's take some bozo who has used our product. Some putz you wouldn't pick out of a crowd if you were staring right at him. Get him to do a testimonial on our product. At some point, he'll most likely say something totally mindless. When that time comes, we'll take that completely insignificant quotation and put it up on the screen underneath him with his name at the end of the statement. People at home will say to themselves "This is the stupidest commercial I've ever seen"! But it will stick in their minds and they'll never be able to forget it. Years from now, someone will be watching TV and say what a dumb commercial they are showing. And whoever watched our commercial will reply "No, it's not the dumbest. There was this one commercial for CholestOff...". The name of our product will ring in the ears of everyone within hearing range and sales will continue year after year based on a single commercial!

For some reason I don't think that's how it really happened, but I'm sure the CholestOff executives appreciate the vote of confidence.

On a similar note, I can't help but wonder about this one. I drove past Walgreen's a little while back (Walgreen's being the criminal drug store equivalent of the equally criminal department store, Walmart) and across their electronic sign it read "Welcome Giant Eagle Pharmacy Patients"! Giant Eagle is the local high-end grocery store in western Pennsylvania and vicinity who has a pharmacy. And I thought about it. Basically what you had here was Walgreen's saying *"Hey! Giant Eagle sucks balls! You should get your prescriptions filled here instead"*! What fucking nerve of these executives! Is that unethical? Yes, it is. But then again is it brilliant? Unfortunately, yes, it is. I don't know whether to throw up or buy stock.

There's one product I think marketing fucked up on. At least in my opinion, this is one product I would refuse to buy based on the name itself. I don't give a hot lunch if it's the miracle drug of the millennium, I'm still not buying it. It's called Legatrin. Isn't that the most astoundingly piss poor name you have ever heard of? I could drop a deuce with more creativity than it took to come up with that name. I have a hard time picturing the board meeting. How is it that your company has a pill that research and development proved is effective, that the FDA gave the green light on, that all systems are go on production and you have to come up with a name...and the best you can come up with is fucking "Legatrin"?? I wouldn't consider it a bad name if the suit-and-tie, blow-dried jackoffs were tossing it around as a joke.

You need to have a little fun on the job, understood. But I don't think that was even the case here. I think one of these morons seriously said *"Hey, let's call it Legatrin! Leg-, because it's good for your legs, and -atrin because it's a pain reliever, like 'motrin'. Leg-a-trin!"* It might have ended there if just one of the 6 or 7 remaining Armani-clad boneheads had said *"You know, Bill. That has got to be the stupidest fucking name anyone has ever come up with for anything! 'Legatrin'?? Are you fucking high?? Clean out your desk, you're fired"*! But amazingly, and stupifyingly, that didn't happen. All the other middle-management douchebags just sat there and went "Okay. Legatrin. Yup, yup, yup". Jesus. None for me thanks. What's the next product name these schmucks are going to come up with in their brainstorm sessions? How about a cardiac medicine called 'Heartatrin"? Perhaps a hemorrhoid cream called 'Assholinol'. And to think, someone got paid for coming up with that shit.

SIT-UP AND BEG

There are so many products out there that companies hock to help you tighten your abs. I can save you a lot of money on that shit with one simple secret.

All you need to do is, when you're driving, tilt your seat all the way back into the reclined position. Then when you drive, simple keep yourself upright the way the seat would be holding you. With the starting, stopping and acceleration, you'll use those muscles like you never have before.

True, it may not be the safest thing in the world to do. But fuck it! Do you want safety or do you want rock-hard abs??

BREAKFAST AT THE PRECINCT

Here's a term I've detested since the first moment I heard it: Continental Breakfast. This is one of the biggest euphemisms in our language. It's a big important sounding term for what boils down to little more than fucking coffee and donuts. Yet people who are serving this low budget shit think everyone will be impressed if they call it a (be sure to gnash your teeth when you say it like a wealthy socialite) "continental breakfast". How stupid have we become as a population that we continue to use this ridiculous terminology and think we're fooling anyone with it?

Continental breakfast. What fucking continent are they talking about? They can at least be specific. Is it Africa? South America? There are only 7 to choose from. Which one is it?

When I hear the term breakfast, I'm looking for eggs, bacon, sausage, and pancakes or waffles. At the very least! It would be nice to also have toast, juice and an assortment of fresh fruit. But as far as I'm concerned, if eggs aren't a part of the meal (and I'm not speaking as an ingredient. I mean as a main standalone item.) it isn't fucking breakfast! Scrambled, fried, poached, sunny side up, Benedict, I don't give a fuck. There had better be eggs in some pure, recognizable form.

So back to my earlier point, what fucking continent is it that has donuts, but doesn't have eggs? Going with the "eggs as a pastry component" argument, it's an impossibility. And as far as importing donuts goes, that's bullshit too. If they can import donuts, they can import eggs just as easily! If we're shipping donuts to Antarctica, we can damn well put eggs on the same truck. And Antarctica doesn't need eggs imported anyway. They have plenty of eggs. True, they're penguin eggs, but I don't give a shit what animal the eggs came from. You could make me a snake egg omelet and I'll gobble down that motherfucker! But whatever you do, do **not** take a plate, put a donut on it (or a bear claw or cruller or whatever the fuck you might call it) and pour me a cup of coffee and tell me it's fucking breakfast! Fuck you! I'll whip out my Jimmy Dean sausage and drag it across your upper lip. There's your breakfast, bitch! Bone appetit!

On a lighter note, here's a joke for you. Did you hear Paula Abdul is opening her own continental breakfast chain? It's called "Drunk 'n' Donuts".

I'LL GIVE YOU NINE-TENTHS OF MY FOOT UP YOUR ASS!

There are certain things outside of the language that have outgrown their usefulness (or were simply never useful in the first place). One of the biggest ones in my mind is the nine-tenths of a cent at the end of every gasoline price. Does anyone think that shit is necessary? First off all, and I'm just guessing this was the turd that broke in the septic tank, imagine you have 2 gas stations right across the street from one another. One is selling gas for $1.50 a gallon (yes, I know what you're thinking. I wish, too, but notice I used the word 'imagine'). The station across the street thinks they're going to be tricky dick and balls and make their price $1.49 and nine-tenth, or just $1.499 since my word processor doesn't have a nine-tenths glyph. Essentially the same price, but to the average person, which if you have been in public recently you know is dumber than a fucking brick, it appears that station #2's prices are cheaper, hence they get more business. Okay, back in the day, I can see that working. It's called making a quick buck off the general stupidity of the public. That is after all the American way. But now, here in the present day, **every** station has that nine-tenths on their prices. So please explain to me what the fucking point of that is! It's completely fucking meaningless if everyone does it. What's the next step? Someone is going to start adding ninety-nine one-hundredths to the price? Don't laugh; I certainly expect it!

But here's one thing I'm ready for. I'm on the fucking job with this one! I'm going to get a hold of a lawyer. Someone knowledgeable about the whole "fine print" element of business transactions. There's certainly a limit on how big print has to be to be significant. If it's below a certain size it ceases to be applicable. And if that's true for printed advertising, there must also be a limit for larger advertising, such as billboards and other outdoor signs. Once I've been informed of the limitations, I'll go around town with a nice heavy-duty tape measure and check the point sizes of each and every gas price posted. When I find one that fails to meet the limit, I'll pull in, scan my debit card at the pump and fill up my car. After making a quick calculation of the number of gallons I pumped multiplied by nine-tenths of a cent, I'll go in and demand to be refunded that amount, making it very clear that the point size of the nine-tenths text is below the legal limit and therefore not applicable to my purchase.

Understand that I realize it will be a maximum of about 11 cents. I know this. However, it's not the amount of money that's important to me but simply the principle. That's how I roll, on **principle**. I also want everyone to be aware that if the minimum wage jackoff behind the counter refuses to refund the amount in question, I'm totally willing to go through the store and reclaim that amount in merchandise. I'll pick up a package of Starburst, take one chew and eat it, putting the rest of the package back. I'll grab a coffee cup and fill it with an ounce and a half of coffee and walk out the door. I think the best plan of action though would be to go through and open a dozen bags of chips and take one chip from each bag. That would come to about 11 cents and it would make everyone of those bags unsellable. Considering a bag of chips at a gas station is about 3 and a half bucks a pop, I'm putting them out over $40 for their insolence! That's the kind of thing that will stick in their minds and perhaps even trigger the notion that having nine-tenths at the end of the gas prices is just plain fucking stupid. If any of you happen to be wondering if I realize I have way too much free time, yes. I'm quite knowledgably of that fact. But then again, if I didn't, this book probably wouldn't exist. Funny how it all works out in the end.

SOUNDS LIKE ARTHRITIS

I'm not sure if this place is still around. It's something of a healthy fast food restaurant (talk about your ultimate oxymoron). The name of the place is Au Bon Pain, which I like to pronounce Oh-Bone-Pain. You can also pronounce it that faggoty French way if you absolutely must. Just be sure to add that hauw-hauw-hauw laugh at the end to make it's authentic. I suppose if I must I can remember my god-awful high school years and recall that it's translated as 'the good bread'. But I got to thinking, what if you only translated part of that name? By all rights, you could have a bondage shop in Canada (which has both English and French as its official languages). And you translate 'Au Bon' as 'The Good' but you leave 'Pain' as simply the English word 'Pain'. All together, your shop would translate to 'The Good Pain'. I think that would be a great business venture since the name is already fairly well known.

So for any of you canuck fucks out there reading this, there's an idea sure to make you millions. You're welcome.

JUSTICE WITH AN IRON FIST

I've thought of a really entertaining way to lower the prison population while at the same time increase the gross national product and stimulate the economy. If you're thinking I'm stealing George Carlin's bit, don't. I have too much respect for him to steal his amazing comedy. While his idea about using pay-per-view for execution is fantastic, as well as Stephen King's *Running Man* idea for that matter, my idea goes in a different direction.

I think the beauty of my idea is that it gives the victims and/or their families a chance for hands-on retaliation. It's almost therapeutic in a way. I'll go ahead and do the pay-per-view idea to start, since the world is so populated with sick fucks willing to shell out money to see things like this. Remember the show *BattleBots*? Two teams of guys (usually a father and son, or in some cases, two dorks with no chance of getting a date with anything not made of polyurethane) would build remote-controlled robots that would go at each other until only one robot was still operational.

My idea is to have one convict at a time face off against a similar robot. The robot is run and constructed by the victim of the perpetrator or the surviving family. For the purposes of determining who constructed the robot, we will give credit to anyone who names the robot. Similarly we could allow 'honorary' family status to a team of engineers from MIT. You put the convict and the robot in a steel cage, laced with razor wire. Then you have the two fight to the death (death in the robot's case naturally being cease of function). You set up a variety of matches for each broadcast, enough so that you can squeeze a good 2 hours out of the line-up. If any convict happens to survive, they'll fight a new robot the following week by a different victim or family. In a case of single homicide, the convict only has to win one week. In the case of a mass murderer, there'll be many more matches to contend with.

Once all victims have had a chance to get redemption, if the convict is still alive, they're set free. Another point of brilliance in this is that the convict will probably be missing enough limbs and flesh that they'll no longer be able to commit further crimes like the ones that put them in prison in the first place. The money made from the pay-per-view, after compensation to the team for robot construction costs, will go back into the justice system, thus lowering the taxes citizens have to pay for keeping these fucking degenerates alive. Lower taxes, lower prison populations, redemption for the victims and low-cost entertainment for all; it's a perfect plan, folks! Now it's up to you to write to your congressman to put it into effect. Go get 'em!

DON'T STRESS. KEY PRESS!

I continually have these invention ideas go through my head. Most of them are pretty bad. Like the vibrating tampon idea wasn't so hot. I thought it would help to make women look forward to their periods. Oh, well. Swing and a miss. However this one I think would be a great invention. I think it will be a fantastic replacement for the executive stress ball. Oh, there was a great one! What the fuck was that anyway? It was like a scrotum filled with sand. Who needs to play with that all day?? If I'm going to do that, I may as well stick my hand down my pants and enjoy the real thing!

My invention is quite a bit different than that. It would be a keyboard with pressure sensitive keys. No, not Keyz. That's me! I'm talking about the things you press when you're typing on a computer. The point of having keys like this is discovered in the effect the key presses have on the main computer processor. The harder you press the keys, the faster the processor would run. So if you're relaxing and playing solitaire or surfing the web, you would just press the keys normally. If you're late to work and you want to finish a letter to a friend before you rush out the door, you just need to hit the keys harder. If you have a deadline of vital importance, something that the boss is going to cut your genitals off if you don't finish it in the next 20 minutes, you just need to slam the motherfucker! Get that CPU going so fast you can roast a fucking marshmallow from the heat coming off of it. Notice that in each situation, the stress is notably higher.

Likewise the physical exertion you're using is both increasing the productivity of the computer but also letting you relieve that stress, not to mention burn off calories in the process!

So the next time you're at Staples or CompUSA, look out for my patented stress release keyboard. Oh, and one other thing: If you're doing your taxes at 11:50 PM on April 14th, break out the sledgehammer. Crisis averted!

THE CLOSET CLAUSE

There's a certain prejudice I've noticed for a while now that I wanted to make a little more realized. It has to do with being gay. I know what you're saying. *Everyone knows that there's a prejudice against gays!* No shit, fuckheads! I know that already. But what I'm speaking of is a much more specific prejudice. A pinpoint stigma so to speak. It has to do with coming out of the closet.

Whenever a celebrity makes their homosexuality known, it's usually big news. But the public reactions can be quite different depending on certain factors. The first factor is male or female.

When a lesbian makes her sexual preference known, at least from my personal view, the reactions tend to be more understanding and sometimes even favorable. Why is this? At the risk of sounding biased, I believe it's because the female body is more accepted and admired. The naked female image is much softer than that of the male. There are gentle curves that are almost artistic in nature. There's typically much less hair on the female body as well. Imagine a woman standing naked, with one hand covering her pubic region and the opposite arm draped across her breasts covering her nipples. You can practically see this as a painting or a sculpture. It's a very classy image. That is provided she isn't sticking her tongue out and making a 'rock 'n' roll' sign with her breast hand while fingering herself with the other. That isn't quite as classy. Hotter than fuck, but not classy. Now let's do the same for the male. Picture him stripped to his bare ass and both hands covering his genitals. Try as you might, you'll probably not be able to see this as classy. If anything remotely favorable, it will be seen as humorous! How many movies or shows have you seen where a guy is taking a shower and the curtain falls down. Or maybe he's swimming in the ocean and the tide rips his shorts off. How can that be seen as anything but hilarious! So that would be Women 1, Men 0 in the nudity department.

Now since I've mentioned swimwear, let's see how beach attire is look upon for the different genders. Let's put a sexy, skimpy bikini on the woman's side of the scale and a man's thong (or banana hammock, if you prefer) on the other. Weight-wise, even though women have twice the regions to cover than the men, the man's outfit tip the scale to his side. How is this possible? For one, it's acceptable for women to leave more surface area showing. In fact she needs little more than two tiny patches, one for each nipple, and a small strip no bigger than a Band-Aid to cover her labia. Then all that needs to be added are a few pieces of string to connect the parts. The man's outfit, while only one piece, needs to have enough material to encase his penis and testicles and at least a medium-wide strip in the back to cover his anus.

Now, the man has more material in his outfit, so the public response should be in his favor.

Let's put them in public and see what happens. The woman gets looks from the men in a favorable manner (a nice way of saying every guy wants to fuck the woman silly) and the looks from the women, while unfavorable, are more based on the principle of jealousy that they couldn't look as good in such an outfit. Overall, there's no major ruckus over her attire and she can lay on the beach and tan without being harassed to cover up. Now let's put our thong clad gentlemen out there. The glances from the women are similar to grade school girls when the teacher referred to a rooster as a cock. Giggling, teasing, and probably a good bit of shock. The men on the other hand are crying out in horror for the man to put clothes on, some going so far as to take sand and rub it in their own eyes to avoid the brutal and nauseating sight. Women 2, Men 0.

While it's becoming abundantly clear that women have the advantage when it comes to being overt in their sexuality, there is one final test: Porn. Girl on girl action is a very popular genre of sexual cinema. Men love watching it (mainly because they fantasize about the girls making him 'a sandwich'), lesbians definitely love watching women getting it on, and there are also plenty of straight women who are intrigued by it enough to view it, or at least don't mind viewing it. About the only group of people with no interest in it is gay men. So what do gay men like? You guessed it: man on man porn! And that's the ONLY group of people who like it! Gay porn makes both men and lesbians want to vomit. And even straight women end up with a strange look on their face. A look similar to when she's in a crowded room and someone lets a silent, yet noxious fart slide, but she can't figure out who did it. Women 3, Men 0.

As should be obvious, a lesbian coming out of the closet has a much better chance for a positive public response than does a man. So while it would appear that I'm saying that men get more heat for expressing their sexuality, I want to get even more specific. You probably don't need any proof that it's harder for gay men to say they're gay than it is for a straight man to say he's straight, but I thought about that and wanted to demonstrate to you how bad it really is. Take two men. They both get up on a stage in front of a crowd of people. The straight one looks out to the crowd and says "I'm straight". The response of the crowd is probably something like "Yeah? So?" Now the gay one stands and says "I'm gay". As you can imagine, there's a lot more activity in the crowd. There's snickering. There's teasing. There's probably a little bit of disgust. But why? Why is there a different and far more negative response for the gay speaker? After all they both did exactly the same thing. They simply stated their sexual preference. Is it because the gay man is deemed immoral? That's just a load of shit, especially with there being more leniency toward gay marriage. Attitudes are getting lighter toward the morality of gay life. What I think is the real issue is that people actually get graphic pictures in their head when confronted with the term 'gay'. They picture two naked, hairy men sucking each other off and there's probably a good percentage who picture one guy penetrating the other anally and getting shit streaks all over his meat pipe. Those are some graphic images, but you can't blame them on the guy who said "I'm gay". All he did was say 2 words. **You're** the sick fucks who concocted the prison rape scene in your head!

Now, let's see if we can't get some kind of balance. Same situation. We'll let the gay guy go first this time. He stands up and says "I'm gay". Same response from the crowd as previously. Now the straight guy comes up but this time instead of 2 words, he has a much more vivid oration.

I'm a heterosexual male. If fact I love pussy! I love to pull out my hairy, sweaty cock and bend a woman over and ram it into her sloppy, wet, gaping snatch. And I love to thrust it in and out, over and over again until I blow my load! A big sloppy load of slippery semen loaded with sperm. Then when I pull out, her sloppy pussy lets the spooge, mixed with her own twat juice, ooze out all over the bed in a big puddle that I'll make her sleep in later.

With all that, guess who will get the more negative response? Right! The fucking gay guy! Isn't that some bullshit?? Here's the straight guy pouring out the most graphic details of sexual intercourse to everyone, and you know what the only probable difference in the audience response will be? A few of the people in the audience get turned on.

Before I close out this topic, I want to narrow the stigma down even a little more. When a gay guy comes out of the closet, there's a good chance that they'll not be harshly looked upon if they happen to be an 'obvious' gay. In other words, when a man who has gay mannerisms, talks gay, walks gay and poses little shadow of a doubt that he's gay comes out, the general reaction is "Duh"! Or put a little more succinctly, "I knew it"!

So if you have a gay male friend who isn't obvious about his homosexuality, and he wants to come out of the closet, be caring and understanding and let him know you approve. God knows the rest of the sick fucking world won't! Fucking pricks!

I HEARD YOU THE FIRST TIME

Hush-hush. You ever hear someone say that? What the fuck is that. It's like when someone is telling you a big secret, something that would be deemed 'privileged information', they say it's "hush-hush". What the fuck is the purpose of using the word twice? It sounds fucking infantile! Like poo-poo or wee-wee! Hush-hush; for fuck's sake, just say the word once! *This information is strictly hush.* Or how about 'hushed' *This is hushed information.* You can even pronounce it 'hush-ed' to make it sound more official. That conveys the message just fine to me. In other words, keep your fucking mouth shut! 10-4, got it, chief! Hush-hush sounds like something you say to a fussy child at bedtime. Fucking hush-hush; talk like an adult, you fucking jackoff!

LAST WE FORGET

Did you ever hear the phrase *built to last*? Car companies love to throw that around. They tell you their cars are built to last. What they don't tell you is what the word 'last' refers to.

That's why I'm here. To provide clarification.

The word 'last' in this particular case is **not** being used as a verb, as in a synonym for 'persevere' or 'endure'. It's in fact being used as an adjective, such as 'final' or 'end'. When they say that their cars are "built to last", they mean they're 'built' to the 'last' day of the warranty. After that, you're lucky if the thing doesn't turn into a fucking pumpkin!

SOUNDS LIKE A PERSONAL PROBLEM

Did you ever gross yourself out? Probably not. I'm crazy enough to be the only person on the planet to accomplish this. Regardless, I did it one time when I was watching Lingo. Yes, more on Lingo. Fear not. I'm not going on another rant here. Not in this paragraph anyway. The principle of the game is that you get a 5-letter word, but they only give you the first letter. Then they give you 5 guesses and each time they tell you what letters you have right and you try to deduce the correct word based on that. So this one word comes up. It starts with a 'P', so I say "Paste". Then, completely unknown to me and my conscious thought process, I open my mouth and say "Pasty Puss"! Sure enough right after I spoke those words, an appropriate visual popped into my head, to which I responded "Ewwww! Oh fucking Christ!". Cause here I'm picturing a vagina plastered with the biological equivalent of cheesecake, though not nearly as tasty. And when you spread the labia, it makes that horrible sound. That sound that your mouth makes when you first wake up after a night of heavy drinking. It's the same sound you hear when you peel off that maxi-pad they package with steaks at the butcher. I almost made myself throw up. I'm just glad I wasn't holding a dinner party at the time!

Well, if that description didn't make you puke, let me try once more. Hopefully, this one will either make you spew or make you laugh your ass off. Possibly both, but be careful not to inhale the vomit. No point in getting a respiratory infection just for reading an anecdote. I was in a relationship many moons ago. It was a relationship in which, well, let me just say she was one of those "sexually generous" women. God bless you ladies, too! She was the kind who would be willing to do things for you even though she herself didn't particularly enjoy it. She would (as you may have already presumed) allow me to have anal sex with her. This one incident was rather early on in our relationship, so she still lived with her parents. One evening we're enjoying some time at her place, it got late and her parents went to bed. Obviously, that means time for some boning!...err...excuse me, intimacy. We're in the living room on the floor. I realize that doesn't exactly sound romantic, but for you nookie noobs out there, it's an easy way to avoid squeaky bed springs. If you're taking notes, that's a good one to know. We fool around for a while. I give her a few orgasms from various uses of tongue and fingers (Remember: a gentleman always pleases the lady first, because you sure as fuck aren't going to do it after you had yours!) Now, it's my turn, so I gently and slowly slip it into her 'backdoor'. When it comes to anal sex for me, I don't need to be back there more than 60 seconds before I'm spent. That's another tip. There's no quicker quickie than the hole that is sticky! Anal Poetry 101. So here I go, starting slow, picking up speed a little, faster and faster, then **boom**, I'm done. I slide my member out.

Now I, to this day, am not 100% sure if it happened to be the position we were in or what factor was involved, but when I slid it out, she blasted this huge, thunderous fart! Bearing in mind that we had only been dating a couple of months, this is about the most embarrassing moment of her dating life. She tries to remain composed while she excuses herself to the bathroom. I know she feels horrible about what happened. I don't want her to be, but something like that really can't be helped. I totally understand her running off like that. She gets to the bathroom and closes the door.

For anyone who is unaware, I have horrible eyesight. I can't see in focus without my glasses unless the object is about 2 inches away from my eyes. I normally don't wear glasses during sex unless the lights are going to be on. In this case, the lights were out and there was only a small bit coming from the kitchen. I'm looking down in front of me and on the blanket I'm seeing this dark spot. It's all a blur to me; it could have just been a shadow. I try to squint to see it clearly, but that's futile so I grab my glasses. I look again and what do I discover the dark spot is? A turd. As fate would have it, gas was not the only thing that flew out of her moments before! Calmly and without hesitation, I shuffle off to the kitchen, grab a paper towel, pick up the turd, take it into the other bathroom and flush it. Before she gets out of the bathroom, I go back to laying on the floor and wait for her.

I think it was at that moment that I realized what a special relationship we had. Any time you're with someone, and you're willing to pick up their feces without ever letting them know it fell out of them, that's when you know you have magic.

DON'T ASK, DON'T TELL

I was at the bank recently, and you know how they have all those signs they put up that start with "Ask us about..."? They always have something like that. In this particular case it was "Ask us about our vacation club". So I figure I'm about saving money and shit, and a vacation is certainly something I can use, so I ask about it. Strangely, I get no response at all. So I ask again. Still nothing, not a fucking word! And I'm starting to get pissed. I do not like to be ignored. So I start yelling "Hey! Your fucking sign told me to fucking ask about your fucking vacation club. So here I am, fucking asking! Give me some fucking information"! No response whatsoever. So I take my money and I take my receipt and I drive off. But I'll tell you something. That's the last time I follow through on a posted suggestion when I'm at the ATM! Fuck that thing!

PUT A RUBBER ON YOUR WII-MOTE

As I just mentioned a few paragraphs ago, my eyesight is for shit. I've been wearing glasses since the first grade, and every year my vision just keeps getting worse. But I did have to laugh at myself once. I was reading some wrap-up stories about the Wii at the Electronic Entertainment Expo (or E3 for you geek-speakers out there), and I came across one story that made my jaw hit the keyboard. There was a game coming out at the time called "Fishing Masters", which was a great idea for the Wii-style of control, using the remote just like a fishing pole. The problem was I misread the story the first time I saw it and thought it said "Fisting Masters". When this registered in my head at the moment, you know damn well I wasn't thinking about a fighting game. Come on, look who you're talking to! Like it's possible for me to overlook a game based on causing vaginal trauma for one about fisticuffs! But the funny thing is this lead me to devise the perfect game for the Wii. A porn star game. Check this out: You play a porn star and it's your job to go from a new, young hopeful just working his way onto the scene to a world-renowned porn star. And with the motion-sensing capabilities of the Wii remote, you could have all kinds of different challenges! You could have one part where you have your finger on a chick's clit and you start by moving slowly in a circle, then as she starts to get turned on, you move faster and more erratically to make her climax. Another challenge would be to control the guy's tongue and you flip the controller up and down quickly to work the love button. Then of course for the main scene, you hold the controller at your hips and you have to thrust faster and faster, but before the meter reaches "Load Blow", you hit a certain button combination to pull out, turn the chick around and shoot your wad all over her face.

That would be an awesome game! It's a shame Nintendo has that restriction on Adults Only games. Oh, well. There's always homebrew!

YOU COULD ROAST A LOT OF CHESTNUTS WITH A FIRE LIKE THAT!

Here's another great idea I had for a product. Well, not so much for a product itself, but for a federally mandated requirement for a product. I know I'm not the only one who's had this idea. I'm sure plenty of people will go along with me on this one. Perhaps not to the psychotic extreme I take it, but still. Have you ever driven by a house with Christmas decorations out, and it's fucking July?? Every year without fail some lazy asshole "forgets" they put out decorations for 6 months after the holiday. Here's where my idea would be useful.

They need to start requiring a dedicated, battery-operated circuit in Christmas decorations. These devices will have a visual sensor on the surface of the decoration to sense light. From the end of January to the middle of November, the circuit will be open only when kept out of daylight. In other words, if the sensor detects natural light (i.e. UV rays) during this timeframe, the circuit closes and activated the device. What does the device do when activated? Wait a moment while I rub my hands together and laugh maniacally.

Okay, within the decoration rests fifty 200 watt halogen bulbs. The closing of the circuit turns these bulbs on, which will quickly increase the heat within the decoration about a thousand degrees causing it first to melt and shortly after ignite. In short, if you put your decorations out after Thanksgiving and take them back in shortly after New Year's (like a decent, normal fucking person) there won't be a problem. However, if you happen to be one of those brainless douchebags who are too fucking lazy to take down decorations once a year, your house will become the equivalent of Michael Jackson's hair in a 1980's Pepsi commercial. Hopefully with you trapped inside.

This would serve a dual purpose. Not only would you raise the IQ level of the neighborhood when these stupid fucks either perish or at the very least have to find a new place to live, but think of all the extra space you'll have when they clean up the charred rubble.

Elbow room, just one more benefit of technology.

LATE MORNING TV KNOWS BEST

A while back, I had spent a good deal of time in hospital waiting rooms as emotional support for a good friend. That's probably some of the most boring time in your life, but it's certainly a test of one's friendship, spending hours in a room with 2 dozen sick and suffering people you would probably cross the street to avoid if you saw them out in public.

Most waiting rooms at least have a television, but it's always set to one shitty network station or another that shows brain-dead talk shows for 14 hours a day. This particular morning I had the displeasure of seeing "Regis and Kathie Lee" or "Kelly Lee" or some vacuous cunt, and the musical guest that morning was some group that caters to really young kids, like the Wiggles or the Wobbles or some other fucking nauseating group that sounds like they've all got Parkinson's. And these jackoffs are singing their happy funshine pants horseshit like "Hey! It's a Wonderful Day" or "You're Special" or some sappy musical diarrhea. The whole time I'm sitting there, the only thought going through my mind is *Can I get someone to change the fucking channel here before I fucking throw up??* The longer I have to listen to this shit, the queerer I am getting! I was convinced that if

I had to listen to that for another hour, I was leaving the hospital and taking a cab to the closest gay bar!

What the fuck is it with kids' music that the only messages they convey are 'everything is great' and 'you're a wonderful person'?? It's a fucking parade of lies is what it is! You want to see how wonderful everything is, switch the channel to CNN. The human race is a fucking embarrassment! What's the first thing they always talk about on the news? Who was shot, burned, blown up, tortured or had a table lamp shoved up their ass in the past 24 hours! Yeah! Everything is just fucking peachy! How about singing some songs that kids can actually use like "Hey, Uncle! Don't Touch Me There!" or "Daddy, Why Do You Drink So Much"? A little reality wouldn't kill the diminutive bastards.

While I'm on the subject of these mid-morning shows, who the fuck is this Rachael Ray twat? When did it become customary to give every obnoxious snatch with a microphone her own TV show? And is it just me or does it seem like Joe Pesci fucked Emeril Lagasse and they had her? Fucking Christ balls! You know, I'm ugly and obnoxious too! Where's my daytime program?

YOU TAKE THE HIGH ROAD AND I'LL TAKE THE LO-HAN!

I know this isn't going to gain me any respect from the people reading this book, but hey! Why ruin a streak? It should go without saying that I, amongst many, **many** others, think Paris Hilton ought to be fucking put to death. If for no other reason than the fact that she's a sleazy, degenerate, petridish-crotched cunt. But she has faded into obscurity for the most part. Someone who hasn't appears about once every other week with some kind of celebrity problem. I'm talking about Lindsay Lohan.

Over the years, we have seen her busted for DUI, possession of cocaine, trying to run down her assistant's mother in an SUV, coming out of the closet, going back into the closet, staying in the closet but peeking out. Let's face it, Lindsay is a busy girl! But the funny thing is, I don't look at her like I do Paris. First of all, have you seen her mug shot? When she had blond hair? Perhaps I'm the only person in the world with this opinion, but I thought she was fucking *gorgeous*! Her hair was long and flowing. Her beautiful blue-green eyes were sparkling (or glazed over. Tomato, tomahto). I thought she was a fucking knock-out! As for the various charges, DUI? I'm not going to bash on that too much. In Hollywood, it's just about a fashion statement nowadays. It's like, *anybody who is anybody gets caught for DUI! You haven't been busted for that yet?? Wait at the bar, wait at the bar.* Plus, I have not driven drunk myself, but I've been in a car with a drunk driver enough times to be guilty by association. So I'm letting that one slide.

Now as for the cocaine charge, again, it's Hollywood. Cocaine to them is like caffeine to us. Try going one morning without coffee! For them, it's the same way, except instead of going down the hatch, it goes up the nose. Again 6 in one, half dozen in the other. Regardless of that, I don't particularly have a problem with people using drugs in general. For my money, if this entire world was constantly high on drugs, it would be a much better place. Nothing would get done, but at least there wouldn't be so much fighting and violence. And the crazy part about that: a lot of that fighting and violence is based at least in part on drugs *being* illegal. When was the last time you got in a standoff with the cops over possession of Tylenol? Or when was the last time 4 people were killed because a Pepcid AC deal went south? Lift the ban on some of the lesser street drugs and you're going to have a major drop in violent crime from Day 1. And I realize that there's going to be a lot of deaths because of people OD-ing. But that's only going to happen to the stupid or careless ones. You've got to let Darwinism run free from time to time. It helps to lighten that strain on natural resources, just like suicide. Seems horrifying, but serves a real global need. Next charge.

Trying to run down her assistant's mother. Hmm, that's a creative one! I'm not going to judge her for that either. Not because it's creative mind you, but because the old bitch probably had it coming. Maybe the hag cut Lindsay off in traffic. I would have done the same thing if I had her kind of money! We don't know what Grandma Moses did, but I have a degree of confidence that she did something to deserve it. After all, who hasn't?

So as a message to Lindsay if she should ever happen to read this, don't listen to all those philistines! There may be a lot of people who look down on you, but I'm not one of them. I think you're beautiful and talented and I love you to death. And if you're reading this while in detox, try to keep your head high, sweetie! Mwah!

YERRRRR OUT!

Remember the revival of the game show "21"? No, not "69"! That's The Awful Show's game! 21 was the show that had all that controversy back in the black and white days about being rigged. The revival was hosted by Maury Povich. With hosting like that, I'm surprised every question on the show wasn't "Are you the father?" But on that game one night, I heard the stupidest comment ever made on any game show. Go figure it was on one of the *smartest* game shows.

The comment had to do with the rules of the game. Apparently, if you get 3 questions wrong (which they call strikes), you lose and the other guy wins the cash. When Maury was explaining the rules, he actually said *"Like in baseball, 3 strikes and you're out of the game"*. What the fuck was he talking about?? "Out of the game"?? Which baseball league is he talking about? Last time I checked the rules of baseball, if you struck out, you just had to wait until it was your turn to bat again. They didn't throw you out of the fucking game! What the fuck kind of game would that be?? While it's nice that everyone on the team would get a chance to play, after 3 innings you'd have to call up the fucking injured reserves just to continue the game! And unless you've got 35 or 40 guys on your team, you won't even be able to finish the goddamn thing! You'd have to be grabbing fuckers out of the stands! *Hey, you! Buddy! Put down the beer and hot dog and go grab a bat!* Fucking Maury! What a douche!

RULES OF ETIQUETTE

I'm not the classiest guy in the world, but there are a few personal rules of etiquette I like to follow. Maybe someday you will too.

#1 - If while eating you drop food on the floor, pick it up and continue to eat it. Nothing shows a lack of class more than wasting food.

#2 - If while eating you encounter a bone or piece of gristle, do not try to remove it from your mouth and discard it. Simply swallow it down with the rest of the mouthful, no matter what the size is. While choking and unconsciousness may occur, it's still classier than sticking your fingers in your mouth at the dinner table.

Maybe when I get enough of these, I'll write another book.

KISS AND MAKE-UP

Here's a little something that has always baffled me. What exactly is the purpose of brown lipstick. I'm cool with the various shades of red and pink and magenta. Even some of the weird colors like green and blue are cool, mainly around Halloween. Otherwise it's a bit freaky. Black lipstick even has it's place. That place naturally being the bathroom cutting yourself while listening to My Chemical Romance. But fucking brown?? I can't think of a single occasion where I would like the woman I'm standing next to looking like she just tossed my salad after I forgot to wipe!

The whole brown concept is stupid to begin with. Call them earth tones all you want, it's still just fucking brown. Like when you go into a woman's clothing store, which typically I don't. Every once in a while I get dragged there against my will by the woman I'm trying to bone. And maybe occasionally to sniff the crotches of the underwear to see if there are any new "flavors" in town. But one thing I've noticed is that *everything* being sold nowadays is brown and turquoise. The turquoise I'm cool with. It's a nice bright color. Shows off the labia nicely when it's the primary color of a bikini bottom. But the brown I can't be attracted to, try as I might. Brown is simply the most horrible color in general. It's the color you always ended up with in art class when you didn't mix the paint right. Even in nature it isn't attractive. You've got 2 things: Mud and feces. There are your choices. Pick one. A brown bathing suit to me holds about as much appeal as seeing a woman in maternity clothes. From my vantage point, there's nothing exciting or attractive about a woman who has obvious been filled up with another guy's semen. No thank you!

THE 80s CALLED. THEY WANT THEIR WARDROBE BACK.

There was one fashion disaster I was a witness to that will never leave my mind. If I took my brain out and soaked it in Clorox, it still wouldn't erase this vision.

When driving one afternoon, I saw a guy on a motorcycle wearing those big mirror sunglasses. The kind Ponch used to wear on TV some 3 decades ago. But that isn't the disaster of which I speak. I saw that just moments before something else. I consider CHiPs to be simply an omen. A sign of things to come.

What I saw shortly after that was something that will haunt me forever. A car coming the opposite way contained what had to be the most fashionally-challenged person on the face of the planet. I should have expected it what with him driving a lavender Ford Escort. Jesus! He was wearing a neon green, tiger-striped tank-top. It takes a lot to throw me for a loop, but I was in fucking awe. I was actually stunned by this article of clothing. I probably had the same look on my face as I would after just getting hit in the head with a cinder block. I had to think for a good 10 minutes if I could imagine anything one could wear that was gayer than that fucking shirt. I couldn't do it; I gave up! Aside from a t-shirt with Richard Simmons blowing Nathan Lane on the front and John Travola and Tom Cruise spooning on the back (a shirt that to my knowledge doesn't exist. At least I sure as fuck hope it doesn't!); without resorting to such screen-printed shenanigans, I can't fathom a shirt gayer than that fucking tank-top.

As if the print wasn't bad enough, I want to make clear that this was not a typical tank top. You wouldn't see a plain white version of it with "Gold's Gym" on the front. This wasn't the type of tank top with the thin shoulder strap that are all too common at the NASCAR races. The ones all the smelliest, hairiest, most poorly bathed men in the crowd wear so you can bask in the aroma of their nose-hair-singeing armpit stench. No, this was like someone took a regular shirt and simply removed the sleeves at the seams. It was like a fucking vest! Gay, gay, cock-smoking, tea-bagging, ass-fucking gay!! Maybe in 20 years, fashion technology will be capable of making an article of clothing gayer than that shirt, but at the present time, that's the pinnacle. I'm just thrilled I could only see him above the waist. I would have had to blind myself had I seen the hot pink parachute pants he was probably wearing.

GO THERE? THEY CAN'T EVEN SPELL IT!

This is a minor thing, but I still want to bring it up. We need to change the name of Kindergarten. We have to be able to come up with something a little better to refer to pre-first grade as. Mainly because, well, it's just a weird word!

Kindergarten is a word of German origin. Now, hold on! I have nothing against the Germans, don't get your lederhosen in a fucking knot. After all my car is German. I drive a Dodge. I know it was built in this country, but part of the name of the ownership is "Daimler". That's a fucking Nazi if ever I heard one. Anyway, this particular word comes from the German meaning "children's garden". What the fuck does sitting around, hearing stories, consuming milk and cookies, finger-painting and taking the occasional nap have to do with landscaping and agriculture??

So, it's obviously time to change the name. From now on, kindergarten will be called "Grade Zero". That just makes good sense. After kindergarten, you go to first grade. And since 'zeroth grade' doesn't quite roll off the tongue easily (and come to think of it, I don't even believe 'zeroth' is a word), there's a great deal of logic in calling it 'grade zero'.

That's one reason for changing the name. I know a lot of you don't like my first line of reasoning all the time, so I've come up with another. This is actually a personal reason, but perhaps I'm not alone. There's a small private school near where I grew up that was along the lines of a prep school before going into the public school system. They had kindergarten through ninth grade. On the sign outside of the place, it was abbreviated as "K-9". So every time I looked at the sign, I thought it was a fucking school for dogs! Like an obedience school! My dog had been pissing on the carpet a lot so one day I took her there to sign her up. The broad behind the counter gave me a strange look...anyway. You get the idea where this was going. My point is: change kindergarten to grade zero. It's just easier.

GOTS TO GET PAID!

George Carlin once examined the phrase "You get what you pay for", saying it should be "You get whatever they damn well feel like giving you". I liked that, but I thought about it slightly differently.

If any of us actually got what we paid for, wouldn't that seem to imply a 0% profit margin. How long do you think a company is going to stay in business with that policy?? Imagine if every company in the world operated like that. The fucking world economy would collapse in one day!

I can't help but think people are fucking high when they come up with these clichés.

GITCHY-GITCHY GOO

I discovered something. And I don't mean I found out something other people knew about. I mean I really discovered it! Anyone who has ever had a cat knows that whenever you pet them, they like to help. I mean, quite often it takes little more than sticking your hand out to pet a cat. They'll walk back and forth and rub themselves *using* your hand. I actually discovered why they do this.

I've been with women who like to touch my face softly when hanging out together. I like that, but sometimes I'm sort of ticklish to it. It's usually when the touch is super-soft. I hate when that happens because it kills the mood when I jump up and start scratching like a flea-infested dog! I don't have the same problem when a woman strokes with a normal amount of pressure. One night, I was being softly stroked and I noticed it was starting to tickle, so instead of scratching, I sort of leaned into the stroke to make the pressure stronger. Just like a fucking cat!! Eureka!!

That's why cats do that! Apparently felines are very ticklish and when you aren't petting them firmly enough, they take the initiative to increase the pressure! So, the next time you're petting your pussy, press harder. Your cat will appreciate it. And I apologize if you got the impression I was taking the conversation in a completely different direction at the end there.

SMILES LIKE TEEN SPIRIT

Denture cleanser. Am I the only one who can see what a complete waste of money this is? I'm not saying that to the people who don't have dentures. Well, that's a waste of their money too, but that isn't what I was shooting at. I'm talking to all the folks with fake choppers.

Think about it though. Why do we use toothpaste? Because otherwise, no woman would come near us! Oh, I'm just full of them today! No, seriously. Why don't we use something like Mr. Clean to cleanse our teeth? The reason is because it's toxic. And it tastes bad, but let's go with the first reason. Makes a little more sense. But what about for people whose teeth don't need to be in their mouth to clean them? Eh? Why would they not be able to use something the rest of us toothed folks can't? I can't see any reason someone with false teeth couldn't just take their teeth out and stick them in a cup with cleaner they already have. And with the wide range of toxic cleansers available, you could easily make them *way* cleaner than people who can't remove theirs.

So for you dentured readers, the next time you're at the store, leave the Polident on the shelf and use the Clorox you already have at home and you'll have the whitest smile in the neighborhood! Just be sure to rinse your teeth off well before you put them back in your mouth. No point in ending up in the emergency room just for listening to something my dumb ass said.

SNATCH 'N' SNIFF

This is something that's probably way, way up on the ladder of Keyz's fantasy scaffold, but it's something that's fun to think about. What if a woman's pussy smell was determined by where she was from, geographically I mean. Say if a woman was from Germany, her twat might smell like sauerkraut. Either that or beer. Maybe let the parents choose on that one. If she was from England, perhaps it smells like tea. Or if she was from Russia, it could smell like borsht. Ugh, that's a bit nasty. I can't imagine eating that when it's an actual food. I'm not sure what Mexican women would smell like, but I'm sure it would be spicy. Women from India would naturally smell like curry. Actually on that one, I have a hunch they already do. I would never risk finding out myself. If you have, be sure to let the rest of us know.

But then you could also break it down even further by going regionally. For the United States, each state would have it's own smell. Florida pussy would smell like oranges, of course. It could smell like grapefruit, but you want to be careful it doesn't squirt you in the eye! Maine pussy would smell like lobster. Quite a delicious smell, but be sure to watch out for the crabs (Ohhhh, quit your moaning! I already know that was bad)! Actually if you wanted crabby pussy, you would probably be best to visit Maryland. California pussy, I'm not sure what it would smell like, but who gives a fuck! The way some of them look, I would eat it if it smell like rotten caviar! Just pinch my nose and go to town! Another one that's a mystery would be New Jersey. If I had to guess, I'd say it would smell like Newark. That might not be fair, though. No one in their right mind would go near any pussy that smells that bad!

THE JUICE IS LOOSE

Have you seen the commercials for Florida Orange Juice? Can you tell me why we have these? When I go to the grocery and I want to buy orange juice, I don't go through the different brands and say "Uh-oh, this isn't from Florida. I don't want that". Nor do I say "Eww! This shit's from Florida! Get that out of here. Where's that South Dakota orange juice?" It's juice for Christ's sake. Milk is the same way. I don't give a shit where the fucking cows are from! It's goddamn milk! You know what brand of juice I look for? The one that's on sale! I don't give a fuck if it came from Cuba! The poor section! Shit, I'm probably going to be adding so much vodka to it, I won't even be able to taste the juice.

That does remind me of one commercial that pissed me off from them. I know what you're saying. *Aww, no! Not more commercials.* Hey! If you don't like it, stop reading! I don't really care. As long as you paid for the book, I'm happy! But, don't worry. I almost have them out of my system.

Anyway this one commercial had a bunch of kids at a birthday party. All kinds of shit going on. I think they had a clown. There was cake and ice cream of course. And a few seconds in, they showed what was either the ugliest little girl in the world, or it was an ugly midget dressed like a little girl. And if you're saying *"That's mean! Kids aren't ugly!"*, bullshit, Pancho! About one out of every 4 kids are cute; the rest of them aren't. If you look at your kids and think they're cute, there's about a 75% chance you're wrong! Deal with it. This kid in particular was atrocious. And that's not the worst part. This little spore is washing her hands in the punchbowl. I'm thinking *what is she? Some kind of retard?* People are drinking this punch and this little simplex is polluting it with her nasty little germ-covered hands! The little bitch could have just picked her nose! She could have just taken a dump and didn't wash her hands! If I was the host of the party and I caught her doing it, I would have taken one of those badminton rackets and hit her upside the head with it. Here I am working hard on making the refreshments and Little Miss Cuntface is contaminating it with boogers and anal residue.

So the commercial continues and they show a kid hitting a piñata. When it breaks, instead of candy, all this celery falls out. And the kids go fucking bananas. Not in a bad way. On the contrary, they're thrilled. *Yay! Celery!* The message of the commercial was, if your kids liked what was good for them, keeping them healthy would be easy. Then they say some shit about kids liking orange juice and it being good for them. Or some shit. I'm not big on following the messages of commercials. I'm looking for women in spandex. When a commercial doesn't have a nice hot camel toe, I'm not interested.

So they come to the end of the commercial. Just when you think you've gotten away from the favorite in the Miss Homely Child USA pageant, the little pig comes running up to the camera and sticks her baboon-ass-ugly face in it. Oh, I have never wanted to punch a little kid so much in my life! That disgusting little shit! I was so fired up, I hoped that the parents of this turd-in-pigtails would get third-degree burns on their genitals. It would teach them a lesson for putting the ratface snatch on television. Then I would take the brat, grease her head up, and jam her straight up the director's ass. Right up to her ankles.

God damn it, that pisses me off! You can't show a beautiful woman's vagina, not even on nighttime TV. But they can show some ugly little shitwhore at all hours of the day. If it weren't for screwdrivers, I would stop buying orange juice just to make a point. Maybe I need to switch to bloody marys. The tomato people haven't pissed me off yet.

SERVING A LIFE SENTENCE

The English language is full of annoying redundancies. I'm sure you've heard this one. It has been getting under my skin for years. Whenever someone wants another guy to do something, but the guy doesn't want to do it, they'll throw out the threat "If you don't, I'm going to make your life a living hell". This is at the top of the list of poorly thought-out clichés. If you're ever in a situation in which you find it necessary to use this phrase, don't say "living hell". The word living is completely unnecessary. Just say "I'm going to make your life hell". It's clear and concise. The fact that the person is alive already implies that it will be a living hell. What other option is there? A dying hell? That just doesn't make sense.

The word "life" has long been abused by stupid people who are trying to sound clever. It's totally out of fucking hand. The vilest of grammar criminals are musicians. Lyricists specifically (so all you bass players, just chill). I have a bitch coming up a little later in the book about cookie-cutter,

Mother Goose lyrics some of these hacks get away with. I've got plenty to say about that, but for now I want to focus on one singer in particular: Jon Bon Jovi. Jon, you're a lyrical felon! You come up with the most asinine, brainless vocal swill ever to dribble out of anyone's mouth. Your song "It's My Life" should be enough to put you away for 15 to 20 in musical jail. Let's examine this piece of shit that makes Green Eggs and Ham look like fucking Macbeth. Repeatedly throughout the song you use the line "I just wanna live while I'm alive". So tell me, dipshit. What's the fucking option? When you're alive, you live. When you live, you're alive. When you're dead, you aren't alive. When you're not alive, **you're fucking dead**!! Asshole! You don't need a PhD from Johns Hopkins to figure that shit out! Jesus Fucking Christ. Tell you what, fucktard. Here's some new lyrics for the beginning of that song. *This ain't a song for the brokenhearted. Keyz has written better lyrics* **when he's farted**! How do you like that, cockbag? Maybe you should just *runaway*, you bubblegum-pop singing bitch!

YELLOW, I LOVE YOU

You know how they call the one business directory "Big Yellow". The book, not the website. Yes, at one time we had books full of phone numbers that people used before the internet. Some people still use them. Some people also wear pacemakers. Sorry, I lost track of my thought.

Anyway, Big Yellow is the name of business phone book from Bell Telephone or AT&T or one of those companies. On my way home a while back I think I found a new definition. In Pennsylvania, road construction is about as common as fucking air. You can't drive a mile and a half in Pennsylvania without having to merge from one lane into another because your lane is being "worked on" by the department of transportation. Back in the day, the workers used to wear those reflective neon smocks, but somewhat recently they have changed to wearing plain neon yellow shirts, at least in the summer. I guess they were more comfortable or something.

At the begin of construction when there's only one lane going each way, they usually have a woman holding a sign that says "Stop" on one side and "Slow" on the other. It's always a woman because we here in Pennsylvania stopped our sociological progression in 1842. I'm still figuring out how women get away with voting in this state. In this particular case, the signholder was this huge fucking bull-dyke of a woman. Bigger and more muscular than 90% of the guys working the road! This is the kind of woman who makes Rosie O'Donnell look like Hilary Duff. And she, like the rest of the construction workers, is wearing one of the fluorescent yellow shirts. Either that or a tent. I couldn't be sure at the speed I was going. I looked at her and said "Fuck the phone book! THAT is Big Yellow"! God-diddly-fucking-damn! In all honesty, I don't think she needed the sign at all. She could have just walked out to block the traffic. That monstrosity could have stopped a fucking 18-wheeler in its tracks!

FAMILY FRAUD

I realize of the 4 people who will ever read this book, chances are 3 of them aren't big into game shows. For the other guy, you probably watch them for the same reason I do; because you like a program that makes you think and that stimulates your brain instead of just sucking the intelligence out like every other type of show on TV. Regardless of whether you're a game show watcher or not, everyone has to have caught *Family Feud* once or twice in their life. I don't care if it was with Richard Dawson, the guy who hung himself, that fat ass Louis Anderson or the new guy with gray hair. No one is capable of steering clear of that show entirely their whole lives.

There's one part of that show that has remained consistent throughout the years. When the host comes around to the different teams and asks the lead to introduce the family, they always piss me off by editorializing. Every fucking time the head douche goes down the line of low-frequency losers adjacent to them, they have to use a seemingly endless stream of adjectives to describe these dumb fucks.

*Hi, I'm Milton! This is my **lovely** wife Doris. This is my **handsome** brother Gordon...*

And so on until he reaches the end of the tard parade. And I want to lash back! You know what, motherfucker?? Keep all the 'lovelys' and 'handsomes' and shit to yourself. I'm not fucking blind. I can see right in front of me how grotesque your family is. You lying about it isn't going to change the cruel genetic plan nature had in store for them! I don't need you giving me your worthless, jaded opinion about this cavalcade of douchebags! That sasquatch you call Doris? There's nothing 'lovely' about her. She has four dozen moles on her face and the gap between her front teeth makes it look like she needs a fucking clothesline to floss. I wouldn't fuck her with Ray Combs' dick! And as for Gordon, is he a hydrocephalic or does he just have an enormous fucking head?? You put a wig on the motherfucker and it looks like a fucking furry yarmulke! Jesus Christ! Where did you get your family? At a fucking petting zoo?? Leave the fucking editorial comments out of the introductions, will you? Or at least use a little honesty in them.

This is my smelly whore of a wife Doris, who is fucking the Puerto Rican FedEx guy while I'm at work. This is my abusive, alcoholic brother Gordon, who is out on parole after taking a shit in the collection plate at church.

That information is a lot more useful! It would certainly explain a lot more when it comes time for these degenerates to play the fucking game.

And while I'm on the whole editorializing thing, let's talk about these jackoffs who do the news. The great Mr. Carlin shared my view on this as well. What George failed to mention was the weatherman's reports. The phrase "Today is going to be a beautiful day" should never be spoken from a weatherman's lips. For the record, I don't call them 'meteorologists'. That title seems to give them way too much credit for what they do, which is standing up there and guessing what the weather will be like tomorrow. I can guess at my job too, but it would probably get me fucking fired. These weatherfucks could basically do their job with a fucking dart board and a handful of Post-It notes! Anyway, I'll save that for another time. What I'm talking about here is their need to editorialize during their segment. If I walk outside and they sky is filled with millions of floating spandex-clad supermodels, then I'll be the first to admit that's one fucking beautiful day! But chances are all I'm going to see is the fucking sun! This may come as a shock to some of you, but where I come from 85 degrees and sunny is not a beautiful day. For one thing, it's too fucking hot. Just about anything above 75 makes me sweat. Can we all agree that the thought of my fat, sweaty ass is anything but beautiful? The other part of that revolves around the fact that we don't have a fucking ozone layer anymore. So what you have is a bombardment of cancer-causing radiation pounding anyone who is so bold to step outside of their house. Not to mention sunburn as well as the second-degree burns you're going to get from your car's upholstery when you sit on it in shorts.

Here's my idea of a "beautiful" day. Overcast, maybe a light drizzle, temperature in the high 60s. Strangely enough, this is the type of day the button-down weatherturd describes as "miserable". What the fuck is miserable about it?? Rain is very cleansing. It cleans the air as it falls through the sky. It waters the plants and trees. The ones that produce a little thing called **oxygen**. And yes, they need sunlight too, but they get that when it's overcast, and they don't have to worry about drying out so easily.

And to wrap this up, I do want to throw a stab or two at the news anchors for the use of "thank goodness no one was seriously injured". Let me tell you fuckers something. Presenting a story about a car crash where the drivers suffered minor injuries is not news, and unless it's an amazingly slow news day, it probably won't even be mentioned on your cast. However, if there's a 6-car pile-up where bodies and parts therefrom were thrown 30 feet in every direction, you can be damn sure that's making the #1 story! If there's an explosion in the gardening section at Home Depot and there are people running around with rakes and shovels going in one orifice and exiting another, you cocks probably won't even be able to hold it until the 6 o'clock cast. You'll be shoving that at people as soon as the clock hits 5!

So don't give me that shit about how you're thankful people weren't seriously injured. Serious injuries make your ratings rise, fuckers! If you offer that sentiment on a lesser news story, either you don't mean it and you're a fucking liar, or you mean it, in which case you shouldn't even have a job doing the news. If you care that little about your popularity and your ratings, you should be flipping burgers somewhere, you apathetic cunts!

EAR-GASMS

Here's another of my fine invention ideas. I think this one would go over big with people who are into Zen and meditation and such.

This invention would be in the form of a helmet. Much like a football helmet, this one would have holes where the ears are. In each hole would reside a tiny 3,000 rpm motor, and what you would do is take a cotton swab and put it in each motor, fitting it so one end on each side rested comfortably in your ear canals. Then via remote control, you could make the swabs spin inside your ears, being able to control the speed.

Have you ever done that? I don't mean build a helmet that does that! I mean take a cotton swab, stick it in your ear and spin it with your fingers. I'm sure there are a few people who can't stand that feeling, but if you're anything like me, you feel like you're going to come in your pants when you do that! That feeling lies somewhere between sex and morphine for me! And much like an orgasm, I uncontrollably make some pretty funny faces when I do it. I think the look on my face would be like it would if you disconnected my brain.

But imagine what a great idea that is to put into mass production. And the pitch would be so easy. Your commercial would show a woman coming home from work. You could use a guy, but since this is my fantasy commercial I want the vaginal factor involved. She lights some incense and a few candles, puts on some soothing music, and the helmet goes on. She starts moaning and rubbing herself, breathing heavier and heavier. Then she starts crying "Yes! YES!", then as her body quivers...oh, wait. Hold on a sec. Whew! I just got myself a little over heated there. Well, that commercial can be tamed a little for network audiences.

GO TO HELL...ON WHEELS

This is a word of advice for all you motorcycle driving fuckers out there. Just because you think that drivers should be more careful around you since you don't have the safety of a car or truck on your journeys, doesn't mean it's going to fucking happen. I'm sure driving a motorcycle is fun, but like any other type of fun, there's always an assumed risk. Especially if any of you get near my fucking car!

If you see my car in front of you, beside you, or in your rear view mirror, it's in your best personal interest to steer fucking clear of me. Here's an example of what I mean.

On the way home from work once, there was some douchebag on a bike. That's what I call motorcycles normally. If it has less than 4 wheels, whether it has an engine or not, it's a fucking bicycle (or tricycle). And those are nothing but fucking toys. These rules are going to apply just as much to a 5-year-old on a big wheel as they do to some fat, greasy, B.O.-ridden Harley-Davidson rider. For the record, I drive pretty fucking fast, and I'm always in the left lane. I'll talk about that another time.

For now, I want to make clear that this day was a day like any other. I'm speeding along, I'm in the left lane, and I come up on some smelly cocksucker on a bike in the right lane. In front of him is a tractor-trailer. We start going uphill and 18-wheelers typically slow to a crawl on the hills of Pennsylvania. When I'm about 50 feet from the two, the bike-ridding fucktard swerves in the left lane to pull around. Now this unbathed ballsack is probably expecting me to jam on the brakes. It's amazing how taking something for granted could so easily get one killed. I do **not** slow down. I keep right on cruising until I'm about 2 feet from his rear wheel before I even let off my accelerator. I guess that created some fairly chaotic wind turbulence, because his bike started shimmying and shaking from side to side. Not 2 seconds later that motherfucker is back in the right lane. The lane he never should have left in the first fucking place! You don't cut in front of me when you have a Hummer much less on a fucking bike, unless you have some kind of death wish.

If you want to meet your maker, there are few ways of doing it quicker. Otherwise you had better stay the fuck out of my way.

These dumb fucks like to say they drive a *hog*! Well, keep up that shit and find out how long it takes me to turn you into bacon and pork chops, motherfucker!

THE BLAIR SANDWICH PROJECT

This is something I've been fed up with for a long fucking time. There's an east coast pizza chain that used to be called "Pizza Outlet". They changed their name quite a while ago to "Vocelli". Perhaps because it fooled people into thinking actual Italians took it over. At least that's what the Irish guys from the local Chinese restaurant told me. Before the name change, they had some of the best hoagies (AKA subs, AKA grinders, AKA...well, you get the idea). The bread was made locally and it was soft and flavorful and delicious, at least as delicious as one might expect from plain old bread anyway. Unfortunately with the different name came different recipes. They started making the hoagies with this shitty ass focaccia bread. Here's how they make that trash. Take a flavorless lump of dough, coat it with flour, and stick it into the over without a pan. It tastes like shit and it looks like something a blind retard tried to make in arts and crafts. Like a failed ashtray. It's a butt-ugly lump loaf. The old bread had character. The new bread had shattered dreams. I can imagine the dough saying something like "I could have been something. A soft pretzel. A sandwich roll. But no, I had to get bought by fucking Vocelli. Now look at me. I'm a fucking focaccia"! It isn't often I pretend bread has a consciousness.

The first time I tried once of these shit sandwiches, I thought someone had taken one of those big powdered doughnuts, removed the cream filling, removed the powdered sugar and replaced it with ground chalk, pretty much removed all traces of flavor, and put meat in it.

Here's the icing on the cake though (so to speak). Once they made this change, they stopped calling them hoagies and started calling them paninis. I don't know if Vocelli started the trend or if it was merely a coincidence, but it seemed like the word 'panini' exploded after that! It wasn't that places were actually offering paninis, like Vocelli. They simple decided to call what was once a sandwich by the new name. It was like any time someone took 2 pieces of bread and put something in between them, they had made a fucking panini. And I started to get mad and began yelling at people. *It's a fucking sandwich, you asshole!* We have been calling sandwiches *'sandwiches'* for like 200 years. There was nothing wrong with that name. Then everyone thinks they're going to get all trendy and call it a panini. Fuck that shit! I won't even buy them! If the minimum wage jackoff behind the counter wants to sell me a sandwich, I'll buy it. The second he calls it a 'panini', I'm smashing it right in his fucking face and walking off! You want to know the real difference between a panini and sandwich. A buck-fifty! That's it. Otherwise it's the exact same fucking thing! You want a panini, fucker? I'll bake up some nice flavorless focaccia and stick my cock in it for you! I'll call it a *penisini*! Special sauce extra.

THE RETURN OF THE LEATHER HELMET

Here's an idea in sports entertainment that I think would be fucking great! You start up a football league, and when I say 'football' I mean the brown, oblong ball with the stitches on one side and 2 white stripes. The other thing, the round, white ball with black dots on it is a 'soccer' ball. When World War III comes around, I'm pretty sure it will have because you non-USA fucks refuse to call your sport *'soccer'*. We have the bombs – We make the rules!

So you start up an *American* football league with all of the old guys that have been inducted into the Hall of Fame. The ones that are still alive anyway. You suit them up and you call it the GFL, Geriatric Football League. Wouldn't that be fucking hilarious??

You'd have quarterbacks getting sacked and breaking a fucking hip. You'd have a running back get nailed head on by a linebacker and his dentures go flying. Possibly for the first down! I think it would be great for advertising too! All the sponsors would be Geritol and Depends and that fucking Grecian formula shit. That would be entertaining as hell! As long as I can refrain from imagining what the locker room would smell like. It would be like a fucking Ben-Gay factory.

THAT STICKER IS A GAS!

I was coming home from work and I saw what I think is my favorite bumper sticker of all time. Actually it wasn't so much a bumper sticker as it was one of those magnetic ribbons. You know those ribbons that America seems to have overdosed on in the past couple of years. They have them for just about every cause: breast cancer, support our troops, feed the homeless, support gay rights. I've even seen them for all kinds of sports teams. Imagine that! Here's a symbol of hope being used to advertise personal preferences regarding a specific bunch of overpaid, steroid-injected morons. Isn't that delightful.

But since the ribbon symbol was already destroyed by professional sports, I felt at liberty to laugh at this one. It was a plain white ribbon with red trim, and it's slogan was "Support Farting". I'm not big on putting stickers and other shit on my car. I don't even like to put the registration sticker on there if I don't need it, which is usually when I get pulled over. But that's one decoration I would proudly display on my car! After all I'm a BIG supporter of the cause! Both in volume and intensity.

IT'LL B.O.-KAY

I have lots of ideas for laws that need to be passed that we don't have yet. One of my biggest lobbying efforts (and by that I mean I just really, really want it without putting any kind of effort into it) has to do with the use (or lack thereof) of deodorant. How is it that wherever you go, you can always find one inconsiderate cockbiter who smells like low tide on the Jersey shore. The kind of asshole that smells like rancid Ritz crackers. It's a fucking crime, though not yet an actionable one.

Here's what I'm going to start doing. And I hope any smelly thoughtless bastards reading this are paying good attention so you can see it coming. I'm going to start wearing a utility belt wherever I go. Kind of like the one Batman uses. Well, I would be going above and beyond to provide a public services for no pay and little recognition. So I might be considered a superhero of sorts. But unlike Batman, whose belt contains lots of amazing and very expensive gadgets, my belt will only hold two very simple, low-tech cans of Lysol. That way the next time I come across either some smelly prick who has some illogical aversion to a little Speed Stick once a day, or on the other side, some skanky bitch who hasn't washed her pussy in 3 days and has a cloud of noxious, fishy fumes emanating from her crotch, I'm whipping the cans out and hosing said fuckhead down with my disinfecting spray of justice. And I'll tell them, either they learn to utilize the basic rules of good hygiene correctly or they stay the fuck home!

Now, in the chance that the motherfuckers give me shit about my brash approach toward their condition, I'm perfectly willing to pull out the old Zippo and *then* spray them down. If I can't kill the germs with disinfectant, then I'll fucking burn them off with flaming aerosol!

LAST CALL FOR GRAMPA

There was a commercial I remember seeing for Pearle Vision a long time ago. The commercial wasn't anything to write home about, but there was something that stuck with me about it. There was this old guy. And when I say old, I don't mean transistor radio old. I mean fucking Parthenon old! I think he may have been Moses' nephew. He speaks to the camera.

I've seen fire engines pulled by horses. I've seen an American flag with 45 stars...

And he's just going on and on about all the shit he's seen in his 217 years on the Earth. Here's my reply to him. **Get in the fucking box, Methuselah!! You have lived on far too long. You're a life glutton! Kiss your family goodbye and get in the fucking box!** These are the type of motherfuckers who just linger on and on. And they walk around with their little oxygen tanks on their little carts. And they putter around on their little motorized chairmobiles or whatever the fuck they are. And the worst part of if all is these old Metamucil-guzzling pricks are using up resources, both natural and financial. These are the same sons of bitches who lay in a bed for 3 fucking years on life support, draining the family nest egg until there isn't a fucking penny left.

Here's a new rule. When you retire, when you're no longer a productive member of the workforce, you have 5 years to do whatever you want. You've worked all your life, you deserve to go nuts! But after those five years are up, you check into a local hospital and receive a lethal injection. We'll have a nice big shot of morphine ready for you; go out with the buzz of a lifetime! You can arrange any kind of party you want. Have your friends and relatives over. Talk about all the good times and how great it has been to know everyone. I'm sure this idea already has the people at Hallmark salivating; coming up with "final goodbye" cards and little bears and shit, being the emotional leeches they are. Then after the pulse has faded away, you can have the funeral service. The old "two birds with one stone" strategy.

Another great part of this plan: If the deceased happens to be married, their widow/widower will be with them again very soon. None of this hanging around 20 years until their health deteriorates shit. That is of course assuming there's a relatively close age span. If it's one of those Jerry Springer type relationships, then the golddigging cunt can go find another geezer to fuck into the grave. All this will quickly become a natural part of American life. You can give it a catchy name. People have birthdays, so you can call it deathday. No, hold on. That's a little too grim sounding. We have come up with some pretty amazing euphemisms in our society, I'm sure someone will come up with something. But what you have here is a sort of planned organization of something that used to be completely random. I like it when things are orderly.

So what happens if the old fart breaks protocol. He retired five years ago, and it's time for him to go, but he refuses to check in for his shot. We have an option. He can elect to re-enter the work force. Lord knows plenty of them do that already. Have you been to McDonald's lately? Christ on a cracker! I went to one a few days ago, it looked like a fucking nursing home behind the counter! And you know how swift those old buggers are. Fast food, my ass! So we have an out for our old friend.

But what if he doesn't want to go back to work either. Well, then I'm afraid it's time to go Logan's Run on his ass. He'll be hunted down like an animal. We will have a national task force: The Fogie Killers. Again, feel free to come up with a better name; it's not quite my thing. These bounty hunters will go around looking for the wrinkled refugees. When found, they're killed on site. The moment that happens, that person has lost all rights to a dignified funeral. The old fuck is taken to a meat packing plant, ground up, and sent off to third-world countries for use as hamburger meat. We'll get Sally Struthers involved with that somehow.

Now they say that with age comes wisdom. So I know these bastards are bound to try and find a loophole in the system. They'll try to pull some shenanigans like retiring for five years, going back to work for one day, then retiring again. Well, guess what, fuckers? I've already thought of that. There'll be an additional rule in place that says once the elder returns to the workforce, they can't retire again. They'll have to work until the day they die, be it natural causes, an accident, or of course the original concept, the voluntary taking of the needle.

And don't get me wrong, it can be part time work. I'm not a fucking Viking ship captain or anything. There'll be required a minimum of 2 days a week, of at least 4 hour shifts each. That's 8 lousy hours a week. That should be at least enough to pay for their fucking Medicare. But no paid vacation for them. I have to draw the line somewhere.

A QUESTION FOR THE AGES

There's a question (a type of question actually) that has been asked since the dawn of the modern age. It's one you have been asked I'm sure.

If you were stranded on a desert island and you could only have one _____, what would it be?

Often I'll just shrug off the question because it always feels like I'm making a huge commitment. Like some cosmic force is going to call my bluff and one morning I'll wake up in that exact situation. But after thinking long and hard, I've come up with an answer I'm comfortable with.

For whatever item fills the blank in that question, I would make sure it was something I could easily commit suicide with. And here's the reason behind such a grim decision. We're talking about being stranded on a fucking desert island. Alone! No electricity, which by consequence means no TV, no computer, no internet, no modern convenience of any kind. All of these put together mean no porn. Magazines might last you a little while, but c'mon! It won't be long till the sun fades the pictures out. That's if the pages don't all end up stuck together. And the salt water spray from the ocean certainly isn't going to do them any good either. Nah, fuck it. Just put me out of my misery, before I end up talking to a fucking half-inflated volleyball.

FIRED UP DOCUMENTS

Here's another thing I have to get a patent on. If you work in an office setting, chances are you deal with a laser printer from time to time throughout the day. If your company makes you use an ink-jet printer, go to your boss and tell him to quit being such a fucking tightwad! You may use your laser printer to print single documents, but every once in a while most people need to eventually print out a 30 or more page document. Like we're going to print Monty Python scripts on our own hardware! Fuck that! Toner is too expensive. The problem with printing large documents on a laser printer is the fact that, by the time the last page comes out, it's almost on fucking fire! You print a 100 page document, you can cook a TV dinner on the stack of papers when you finish. Or at least thaw one.

So my idea is to make a cooler that can be attached to the laser printer. Then after the pages come out, they immediately pass through the cooler to make them a normal temperature. So when you pick the document up, you don't end up with second-degree burns all over your hands.

That's one things that has always bugged me about those printers. How the fuck does the paper not catch fire in there?? Well, it does sometimes when there's a paper jam, but that paper must be right below the flash point by the time it comes out. It's funny thinking back when they first came out with laser printers. I thought that the printing was actually burn marks in the paper at a high resolution. Good thing HP turned me down for that R&D job.

DUMPING ON CARS AGAIN

Anti-lock brakes have been around long enough now that almost every car that drives off the lot is equipped with them. When you're in your car and you start it up, look for the little "ABS" light on the dash.

I thought it would be pretty funny though for Fords and Toyotas to have an "IBS" light. That would be the one that lights up just before the car shits itself. Come to think of it, they may already have that. I wouldn't stoop low enough to spend so much time in one that I would notice.

STEELING HOME

I haven't rooted for the Pittsburgh Steelers since Bill Cowher made the jump to sitting with JB, Boomer and the other guys at CBS studios. Even if Cowher was still around though, I think I might have jumped ship for a different reason.

For the longest time, the team didn't have a mascot. Most of the other teams had one from day one, but theirs were a lot easier. The Bengals had a Bengal tiger. The Jaguars has a jaguar. In fact any team with an animal name didn't really have to ponder what big-headed furry thing was going to represent them as a spirit booster. Then you had the Steelers. First of all, the term 'Steeler' is pretty far fetched as an English word. One who 'steels'. I can understand one who *steals* but that isn't the idea behind the name. Pittsburgh wanted something to represent the steelworkers, not the criminals in the executive office of the mills! But they have been around so long that there's really no point in debating the grammar of it. They're the Steelers. End of discussion. So a few years back, they decided it was time to come up with a mascot. A steelworker naturally. The only other option was something like a steel girder. That would have been pretty lame. An animated piece of metal. Nahhhhh! Smarter heads prevailed and they came up with a big muscular guy wearing a huge hard hat. What's the deal with the hard hats anyway? Steelworkers are supposed to be these big tough bad asses, and here they are walking around with these pussy-ass hard hats. I'll tell you something. If you can't take a cinder block to the head without crying or getting knocked out, then get back to the kitchen and make me some dinner, Sally! Ha-ha-ha, no. I kid.

So we have the form of the mascot. Now here's where I think the big problem occurred. Instead of the owners and the front office guys and even the players brainstorming about a name for him, they went to (ugh!) the fans! It would have been so easy to just come up with something cool like Iron Mike or Hard Hat Harry or Rod Anvil. Something tough and gritty. Even something like Rusty would have been a step in the right direction, being a cutesy sort of double pun. But when they put it in the hands of the general public, we all knew this wasn't going to end well.

Sure enough the fine sports fans of Pittsburgh came up with a name. And it is...drum roll...Steely McBeam! Jesus...Fucking...Christ. What fucking loser picked that name?? I want an address so I can pay a visit to this asshole and thank them personally for adding yet another reason to be embarrassed for living in Pittsburgh. And by thank, I mean beat him within an inch of his life, but I'm pretty sure you already knew that. Steely Mc-fucking-beam. That would be like the Bengals naming their mascot Orangecatty McStripes. It sounds like a fucking sandwich for fuck's sake. *Yeah I'll have the McBeam Deluxe with fries and a root beer.* I can see that being available at McDonald's. Limited time only. Or limited IQ for the stupid prick who came up with the name. It wouldn't have surprised me if the first day the mascot was introduced, he didn't come out. He just sat in the tunnel, crying to himself. *Why did they give me such a stupid fucking name!* Steely McBeam. It sounds stupider every time I say it!

I would expect a name like that for a Cleveland mascot. Christ, look at their football team name. The Browns. Not the Cougars. Not the Grizzlies. Not even the Dawgs, like they imply themselves to be. The fucking Browns. It's a fucking color for the love of anal bleaching!! And not even a good color! It's the color of feces! It sounds like they shit their pants before every game! And by the look of their uniforms, perhaps they actually do! I can't help but think that 'Browns' is actually short for 'Brownstains'.

NICE PLACE TO LIVE...IF YOU'RE A VEGETABLE!

While I'm on the topic of Pittsburgh, I want to point out that not everything there is bad. As far as culture goes, it's one of the finest cities you can visit. It has the symphony, the opera, a museum, an excellent zoo. There's plenty to see if you ever happen by. There's one place that I visited that didn't quite blow up my skirt though. Yes, I'm wearing a skirt right now. I stopped typing just to put it on so I could use that phrase accurately. That's the beauty of writing a book. You can stop whenever you want to take a break and no one ever knows. They just keep on reading. There, I took the skirt off again. You didn't even know until I said something. What the fuck was I talking about? Now, I have to backtrack and read what the fuck I just wrote.

Oh, yes! The place I visited. It's called Phipps' Conservatory. It is, how can I put this? If you get wet/get an erection (whichever happens to be applicable) by studying plants, this place will give you multiple orgasms. This is pretty much the botanist's Woodstock. The way they have the place set up though is kind of funny. It's almost like a maze. Not as intricate as the hedge maze in The Shining, but it's still pretty complex, with all kinds off walkways and pathways and hallways and such. That's a lot of ways. By the way. I'll stop now. The best wa...method I can use to describe it is to take about 50 of those hamster tunnel sets, make them about a hundred times bigger and turn it into a greenhouse. I think I ended up spending as much time trying to find my way out of the fucking thing as I did looking around in it.

What concerned me was that the last 10 minutes, I didn't sweat. I don't mean I wasn't hot. I just mean I had run out of sweat. If I had spent too much more time in that fucking place, they'd have had to take me out on a stretcher. And **that** would have taken a half hour! But the conclusion I came to was actually a quite logical one. The reason why the plants thrive so well in that place is not the heat and humidity. It's because they take the corpses of all the fucking people who couldn't find their way out and use them for mulch! I think it would be interesting to see if there are a disproportionate amount of missing persons reported in that area. Or at least missing botanists. One things for sure. When archaeologists go digging through that area 10,000 years or so from now, they're going to find a fucking mother load!

PREFERRED WALMART CUSTOMERS

A few dozen pages back I discussed a male fashion travesty. As it turns out, men don't have a corner on that market. Understand that I don't have fashion sense. I don't dress bad per se. I wear plain pocket t-shirts and jeans every day. And that's pretty much without exception. I don't dress up. When I go to a funeral, I wear a black T. When it's St. Patrick's Day, I wear a green T. I like to keep things simple and I don't risk going outside of that comfort zone. But a woman asking me "Does this top go with these pants?" is like her asking a retarded chimpanzee. In fact, the chimp might give her a better answer, say in the form of throwing shit at her. My answer is, and always will be "it looks fine". No fucking help whatsoever!

But I do know enough that certain things should be worn by certain age groups. For example, anyone collecting social security should not be wearing those pants with the seat residing right around the person's knees. Those people should probably have their waistband right around their nipples. Now that I think of it, that's probably wear that trend started. Someone had the presence of mind to realize old people wear their pants very high and by inverse, they came up with the idea of young people wearing their pants much lower than they should be. It still doesn't look good, but at least there's a logic to it!

But like I say, women are not immune to fashion mistakes. This particular foe pa (yes, that's misspelled. I know it's supposed to be faux pas, but you know how I hate the fucking

French!) involved a late-middle-age woman. I think that's probably being pretty generous. Bare knuckles, the woman was in her late-50s. The skin wasn't quite falling off the muscle, but it was definitely not holding on by much. She was wearing this skimpy baby-doll type t-shirt, which on the front of it had, in fancy sparkling green letters, the words "Bling-Bling". Here's a grown woman, who has no doubt achieved grandmother status, wearing a shirt that's intended for a girl no older than junior high school age. I'm positive that's where she got this fucking thing. She went into Walmart (obviously a home away from home to this nightmare), into the Junior Miss section and bought this shirt. My guess is, she probably bought several, each with a different revolting insipid saying like "Oh No You Didn't!" or "Talk to the Hand!" or some stupid psuedo-Ebonic horseshit. And I try dare not imagine what else she got there. Like the low-rise jeans. The ones that show off her tramp stamp she got when she turned 42. Well, the jeans attempt to show it since the skin migration had relocated it somewhere near the bottom of her thighs. Of course you can still see her brand-spanking-new thong sticking out. The one around which her floppy saddle-bag labia are dangling on each side. I think I just tasted my dinner again.

What does it say about a woman when she has to raid her granddaughter's closet before she goes out in public. To me it says one of two things. She either is terrified by the passage of time in relation to her age. But more likely it's another reason. I've had voices in my head long enough that I've become accustomed to them, but I got a migraine from the "Trailer Trash" alarm that was going off this time. If she didn't have long hair, I'm sure I would have seen that her neck was redder than the fucking Kool-Aid guy! Oh, Yeah!

BRIDGE OVER THE "LIVER? WHY!"

I'm thinking this is mostly a southern thing. I don't see them offered too much around the north. If you go to a restaurant in the south...wait, scratch that. If you go to a greasy spoon in the south, it isn't uncommon, on the menu, to see the item "chicken livers". Why do we as a people constantly feel the need to take the most grotesque parts of the animal and turn them into "delicacies"? Who eats this shit?? It's a fucking blood-filtering organ for Christ's sake! Whoever is ordering this kind of thing that doesn't belong anywhere but possibly the worst kind of cat food is someone whose breath I don't even want to imagine.

And when you're taking organs from animals and eating them, why be selective about it? You have already crossed the line at that point! Why not fix yourself a nice big helping of chicken kidneys. We have kidney *beans*. C'mon you human garbage disposals, go for the real things! And don't forget the great home-cooked goodness of deep-fried chicken pancreas! Look for that next time you're in the south! Right on the menu: Chicken Pancreas with Sausage Gravy, $4.75. Comes with Grits and Greens. And just to be absolutely positive I've taken this beyond both ridiculous and ludicrous, let's replace those boring sides of pasta with a hearty bowl of chicken arteries! Mmmmm! That's good eatin'!!

Oh, lordy, I can just hear a few of you out there now. *Keyz, you sick bastard! You just made me fucking puke!* But to be perfectly fair, there are few books in the world that double as both entertainment and as a weight-loss aid. Bonus!

This is a totally unrelated point, but it seems appropriate since we're discussing the south. First of all, I'm not what the average person would consider a redneck. I can't stand country music. I don't drive a pick-up truck. I bathe. But despite all of this, I do watch NASCAR from time to time. There's this one crew chief for one of the more popular drivers, Jeff Gordon, and his name is Steve LeTarte. Sounds like a French pastry when you read it. But the funny thing is when they pronounce it on the casts, and this is probably due to the horseshit they have in their mouths, it sounds like 'Le-Tard'. I bust up every time I hear that. That pastry just became a French guy with Downs Syndrome. And if you have ever seen or heard this hillbilly fuck, you would know that it's one of the most accurate, unintentional descriptions of a person ever spoken. I realize that had nothing to do with eating country-fried chicken gall bladder, but well, there it is anyway.

SMALL, MEDIUM AND HOLY SHIT!

I like to go to places like Ponderosa and Golden Corral. Buffet-type restaurants. Bonanza still has a few locations around. Any place that sounds like a bunch of hicks sitting around eating beans from a tin plate, chances are it's a buffet restaurant. I like them not necessarily for the 'all-you-can-eat' aspect, though that's nice too. But I like to people-watch sometimes. A buffet-style restaurant has provided much entertainment to me over the years.

Before I say too much, I know that I'm no light-weight. I'm a big guy, both in height and girth. But when I got into a size 42 waist, I actually did something about it. Mainly in the form of exercise. That was my limit, but I realize when I go to Ponderosa or Old Country Buffet, there are people who have either passed their limit and didn't look back or they never had a limit in the first fucking place! These are people who you just know are regulars to the buffet circuit. Some of these zeppelin-sized motherfuckers must clock in at 450 or above. It baffles me. Where do you draw the line? I can't help but think these fat fucks drew the line in chicken wings and Swedish meatballs and then ate the son of a bitch.

My opinion is this. Whenever a standard bathroom scale is no longer able to tell you your weight, it's time to put down the Twinkies. And I'm not talking about using numerical trickery to get your weight from the scale either. Some of these planetary-looking bastards will tell you that you take the number the scale comes up with and you add the maximum that the needle passes the first time. No, bullshit! If you need to do calculations in order to tell your weight on a bathroom scale, (provided you aren't 7 feet tall) you're too fucking fat, plain and simple.

If you're one of the tank-assed folks I described, I want you to know that even though I mock, I do care. And I want you to realize that you're not alone, nor do you have to fight the problem alone. You just need to turn your life over to old J. C. That's right. Your salvation is waiting for you. You'll be healed when you turn your life over to...Jenny Craig. She'll help you regain control. Did anyone think I was going to say Jesus Christ? Really? Look at who is writing this!

Oh, I almost forgot. What are the legs in those chairs at the buffet places made off? If one of those lard tankers were to sit in a chair that look like that in my house, they'd break it like an elephant sitting on a light bulb! Those restaurants must know the type of consumer they're drawing in so they have the legs steel-reinforced or something. Either that or it's petrified wood.

WHAT'S UP WITH THAT SHIT?

I need someone to explain this little language peculiarity to me. Why is "shit" a profanity, and "crap" is sort of but not really, and "poop" isn't at all. It's the same fucking thing! It's feces! The brown mess that comes out of your ass! We have 3 different terms for it...actually, there are a lot more than just those three. Ca-ca, doo-doo, dookie, turd, dump, poo, dirt, stool, manure, plop, scat, bowel, pucky, dung. There we have almost 20 different terms for 1 biological byproduct. And of them, all but one or two can reasonably be used by children, or very immature adults, with no sort of repercussion. The worst kind of response one using these terms can expect is "Eww, gross"!

But you use the word "shit" and lights and sirens go off everywhere! And people go "Oooooh! That's a swear"! Why? How is it that one word can be a swear and another 2 dozen aren't when you're talking about the same exact thing?

There are a lot of different phenomena that have different terms, some profane and some not, but with slightly different conditions depending on the word. Like 'fuck'. That's another word I think needs to be reviewed, but for our purposes one problem at a time. It's possible and somewhat common for people to argue that 'fucking' is different from 'having sex' and/or 'making love'. Most of this has to do with the parties involved. For example, when a guy on spring break in Tijuana puts his penis into a hooker, he would be more inclined to say he *'fucked'* someone. When the same guy 3 years later gets married, he'll *'make love'* to his bride on their honeymoon. 20 years after that, when the wife is complaining to him that he isn't satisfying her needs, he'll *'have sex'* with her just to shut her big fucking mouth.

Another controversial term, while not an "according to Hoyle" profanity, is the term 'nigger'. When a person of African descent is being referred to as either 'nigger' or simply as 'black', there's probably an additional secondary characteristic being addressed by the former. Both may be descriptive concerning his race, but 'nigger' is probably calling attention to an additional feature, such as the way they talk or act. In this case, there's probably also a certain degree of emotionality in the use of the term. Rarely will you hear it being used when anger and/or annoyance don't play a part in the verbal exchange.

So as can be seen, one doesn't need to look too far to understand how different terms can have slightly different meanings. But now, let's return to 'shit'. First off, it doesn't really matter where the shit comes from. With the exception of 'manure' (which generally is used when the fertilizing properties are focused upon), all of the aforementioned terms are interchangeable in spite of what type of animal the shit is coming out of. Human, dog, cat, horse, fish, bird, or even

Rosie O'Donnell. There's no real distinction between any of those aside from consistency and smell. It's all shit. Whether it came from an elephant at the zoo or Uncle Joe in the bathroom after Thanksgiving dinner, a shit is a shit is a shit. So what kind of effect does emotional value have in the term? None whatsoever, nor should it! It's shit. Shit does not have emotions. While it's capable of *containing* very small living things, it by itself is *not* a living thing. For example, if you have two dogs and they each take a dump on either side of the room, you can go up to the first pile and yell at it and say "You are shit! A nasty smelly pile of shit!" then go to the other pile and go "Aww! You're such a cute little poop! Aren't you? Aren't you?" But even after addressing both piles in a very different manner, there'll not be a single change in either of them. Not in color, nor in smell, nor in size. Not one solitary change.

So with all that in mind, I propose that we, for lack of a better word, decriminalize the word 'shit' and let it become part of the group of safe words for feces. The word 'shit' is just as harmless as the rest of them. When your child says "I shit my pants", don't get angry. Just chuckle. Then look at your spouse and say "He called the poop *shit*"!

Well, that's enough of that shit.

SNAIL MAIL DEFINED

I have a feeling I know where these Geritol-poppers, these old fucks that are even to old too work at McDonalds, I think I know where they go after they have finished their years of service at the company who employed them for so long. The Post Office.

I had to mail some DVDs once. Instead of going to UPS (which absolutely guarantees that if you don't buy insurance, your shipping item will arrive totally demolished), I go to the Post Office. When I got to the counter, the combine age of everyone behind it had to be 230. And there were only 2 people working! Christ! Is the United States so hard up for postal employees that they're sending headhunters to the fucking nursing homes?? That must be the governmental balance. The Army sends recruiters to high schools and colleges. The Post Office sends recruiters to retirement villages! These recruiters show up at the rest homes, and since the people in the homes are about to get kicked out for inability to pay (since the orderlies stole all their money), the residents have no choice but to head back into the work force. It's just a suspicion, but I think the fuckers working in the nursing homes are in cahoots with the people running the Post Office. The douche at the rest home robs one of these poor old fucks blind then call the Postmaster. *Mildred Finklestein has two weeks left. Send a recruiter out.* That has to be the way they have things working. Because I buy so much as a book of stamps and these fuckers take 25 minutes to count out change for a ten! Imagine someone behind the counter with a shriveled voice:

Let's see here. That was 8 dollars and 80 cents. Which means I owe you...uhhh...

Then he take a minute and a half to adjust his Coke bottle glasses just to read the display on the cash register. Because god forbid one of these old bastards try to do math in their head. They'd probably blow a fucking aneurysm.

Okay, that's 1 dollar and 20 cents. Let's see, here's a dime. And here's another dime. That's twenty cents. Oh, my. Back when I was young, I could go into a coffee shop and get a sandwich and a piece of pie for that. Now let's see, that was 20 cents and...

And I'm about ready to blow a fucking fuse on this prick and tell him *"Just gimme my fucking receipt"*! Next thing I know the old fucker will be giving me the buck in pennies. And looking at the date on each one, telling a story about where he was that year. I can't believe their aren't more homicides in the Post Office. Not from disgruntled postal workers. From the fucking customers!! Though the experience did explain one thing to me: Why it takes 3 fucking days to get a package from someplace that's a four and a half hour drive away!

A SMELL OF SUCCESS

Here would be a good idea for candle companies. Make scented candles. Yes, I know they already have those, but I'm talking about a much wider range of scents. They have strawberry and cinnamon and vanilla and that kind of thing, but I think they can shoot for a bigger audience. Sweet, fruity and minty will only get you so far as a candle manufacturer. But when I go looking for a candle, there are a lot of good smells I haven't been able to find. Smells like...bacon! I would fucking love a bacon-scented candle. Fire that baby up and it would be like breakfast all day! And don't say "Kevin Bacon"! I don't want my apartment smelling of nasty trailer-trash odor. I'm talking about the pork product. They can't make it from actual bacon grease though. That just doesn't sound safe. The whole fucking building would end up engulfed in flames. And smelling like bacon. No, they need to find a way to come up with a bacon extract and use that to give the candle its scent.

Or, you know what would be another great smell? Homemade vegetable soup! Can you imagine that! Just the thought has me drooling. Now that I think of it, maybe that's why they don't make those type of scents. Because people would be hungry for that stuff all the time. If I had a bacon-scented candle, I'd be wanting it every day. End up with a cholesterol count higher than a Krispy Kreme donut.

CAN I GET A BELCH FROM THE CONGREGATION?

Have you ever been talking to someone, and a belch flies out in the middle of it? Isn't that fucking terrifying?? That you have so little control over your body you can't even finish a sentence without blasting stomach gas? What if it had been one of those belches where you partially throw up? You'd have to get the person you were talking to a moist towel!

But there's still a lot of entertainment value in that type of incident. Like when you do it in the middle of a blasphemy. *Jesus Chr-braaaaaap-rist!* That's some hilarious shit! There are two types of reaction the person listening can respond with. Either laugh to the point of soiling themselves, or simply stare in total disbelief. But this concept lead me to a theological question. Maybe the Catholics can provide an answer for this one. When you belch in the middle of a blasphemy, does it make the blasphemy worse? Or does it possibly void the blasphemy? Here's what I mean.

On the one hand it's like adding insult to injury. Not only did you "take the lord's name in vain", but you had the nerve to belch in the middle of it! That's like, after you kick the barstool out from under a guy for looking at your woman, and after you break the beer bottle and jam it in his neck while he's laying on the ground, and still after you step on his nuts until you hear them burst like a couple of ping pong balls filled with mayonnaise, after all that, it's like squatting down on the guy's face and ripping one of those truly repulsive, half-liquid farts.

Now on the other hand, there's a chance that since the blasphemy was broken up by the belch it may not count. Kind of like not taking your finger off the chess piece when you make a move. It doesn't count. It's like calling for a do-over.

I hope someone with a bible can help me out with that dilemma one of these days. Maybe it will just forever be one of those religious mysteries. But I can't help but think that maybe it was God that made you burp at that precise moment in order to break it up for you. Wouldn't that make sense? I mean to you religious dimwits?

THE RETURN OF "GO MEAT!"

At the beginning of this book, I bashed on Hillshire Farm for their infinitely annoying "Go Meat!" commercials, but I like to give credit where it's due. And on occasion even when it isn't due.

I love a good Hillshire Farm cheddar brot! They know how to make those right. I was making a pack of those one night for dinner. When I pulled them out of the toaster-oven, one of them had split down the side. They were kind of like Ball-Park franks with the plumping action, and much like me and my jeans, one of them will occasionally become too big for its casing and blow out. The problem is when sausages split down the side, they end up looking like a vagina! So here I'm getting ready essentially to chow down on a cheesy, pulpy vagina. Hopefully you didn't just projective vomit all over the book. If you didn't and you can still read this, I'll continue.

But that got me thinking, wouldn't that be a great marketing campaign? You make the brots so stuffed that bursting becomes an expected event. Or you could even make a perforation down the side of the casing to have the same effect. Then right on the packaging you put *Vagina Brots*! Are you fucking kidding?? That's all I would eat! You could probably even do the same thing for women. The ones who aren't lesbians anyway. You could inject a channel of cheese into the sausage that, when heated, would burst out of one end! Then you have *Penis Brots*! Or *Cock Brots* I think has a more poetic ring to it. Let the marketing guys choose which way they want to go on that. But here you would have a little something for everyone and sausage sales would skyrocket! The only problem with the Penis Brots would be that very few women would swallow, but it's a work in progress.

IF BRAINS WERE GUNPOWDER...

What the fuck is up with these asshole rednecks who put fake bullet holes all over their trucks? These stupid inbred fucks! What's the purpose of defacing your vehicle with decorations that make it look *more* like a piece of shit. Just for clarification, it's mostly Fords I see with these things on them, so it's really an exercise in overstating the obvious. But how do things like this even come into being?

Someone somewhere apparently had a lucid thought: *You know what would be really cool? If we made stickers people could put on their trucks to make it look like someone shot at them!* As if that weren't enough, someone must have heard this idea **and** somehow thought it was a good one! That to me is the more amazing thing. People have bad ideas all the time. The standard response from someone who overhears these ideas is quite often, *"What are you? Fucking stupid?"* But somehow in this particular case, that filter failed.

It blows my mind that some people live in harsh and dangerous neighborhoods where gun violence is all too common and not being near gunfire for an entire 24-hour period is a blessing. And then you have these retarded shitkickers buying decals that simulate violence when they live in the sticks and the only gunfire they hear is during hunting season! It would seem the only deducible conclusion is that these fucking toothless morons want people to think they're hardcore because they get shot at. These brainless cretins probably think they're going to get laid when they hang around the back of their truck and women walk by seeing the stickers. *A-yup! I's been shawt at. I's is a bad ass. Other guys shoot at me cuz they caint handle how bad ass I am!*

Let me tell you something, Hopalong Dipshit. It doesn't matter how many stickers you put on your piece of shit pick-up. No woman is going to see those fucking things and say *"Ooh! Wow! You must be so dangerous. I just want to spread my legs for you, right here"*! You fucking hard-on! You know the only thing that's going to help you? Funny, because I don't know myself. What the fuck do you even have to offer a woman other than your poor hygiene and the back of your hand? What you need to do is get a *real* gun with *real* bullets. And don't even waste them shooting at the back of your truck. Try shooting them in the back of your head. Right where your deficient brain stem is. You fucking, shit-eating hillbilly!

Some people have no fucking IQ at all. Like calories in a Diet Mountain Dew. Zero.

COLUMBINE WAS JUST THE START

I've spoken out about population control for several years now. But I'm not just interested in the political incorporation of it. In other words, letters to Congress are a start, but they're not the only cards up my sleeve. There's a lot that can be done just by regular people. Here's an example of what I mean.

What you do is hook up with a really hot looking chick. By hook up I don't mean sexually. That's probably the one and only time I won't mean it that way, mind you. I mean try to get to know one through a friend, a sibling, however. Also, by hot, I mean someone who the average guy would stare at until she's no longer in his field of vision. That way he can have a good reliable mental picture in his head for when he's flogging the bishop later that night. Her relationship to you is not nearly as important as the need for her to be a head-turner. Describe the following plan to her to make sure she goes along with it. Then here's what you do.

You jump in the car and head out to the local mall. Weekends are the best time to do this because they're busy and there are lots of people coming and going at any given time. What you need to make this work is an area that has a clear line of vision for about 75 feet. People will naturally be passing through but avoid poles and structures and kiosks and such. Have her hanging out about 50 feet away from you. She can be sitting, reading a book, inventorying her purse or whatever. What you're going to do is keep your eyes peeled for a really geeky loser. Someone who doesn't quite grasp the concept of regular hair cleansing. Guys who are wearing tennis shoes composed of more than 2 colors, easily visible since their pant cuffs are about 6 inches above their ankles. Guys who wear a polo shirt that it buttoned all the way to the top. Basically a Poindexter from hell. Guys who are on a mission to RadioShack are perfect for this purpose.

As this dork passes you going toward her, follow him closely. When he gets about 25 feet from her, signal her to start waving to him seductively while looking straight into his eyes. Chances are this guy is going to try his hardest to be cool and avoid the temptation to look around for the person she's really waving at. There's nothing more uncool than looking around with a clueless look on your face and going "who me?", and most dorks know this. If you have ever wanted to appear like a total loser, just do this in a public place. You'll be as popular as anal sunburn. Instead of looking around, the target will simply wave back. He may go so far as including other mannerisms to add to the alleged coolness. At that point, you speed up, walk past him looking right at him, and say "She's not waving at you, you fucking dork"! When you get to her, inform her of the dork thinking she was waving at him while pointing directly at him. Then both laugh out loud, continuing to point at him. Call out to him using some classic nerd insults like 'dork', 'spaz' or whatever happens to be the current *in vogue* slang. If you would like, follow him around continuing to mock him until he starts sobbing and yelling "Leave me alone"! The more cruel you are, the better you'll achieve the desired result.

Now, the question is "What's the desired result?" and "What does this have to do with controlling the population?" Okay, two questions. Nitpicker! Here's what we hope to achieve. If done well enough, this incident will brew in Poindexter's head for days and weeks, eating away at his sanity. It will bubble and boil until he completely snaps. At that point, it's hoped that he'll acquire some sort of automatic weapon, go into a crowded place and kill everyone in range until the police take him down. This translates to fewer people, less traffic and more parking spaces. It's a situation in which everyone wins. Well, almost everyone.

Now, there is the possibility that the dork will simply kill himself after this treatment. If that's the case, feel free to write it off as a dud. After all, not every bomb explodes like it's supposed to. Don't be discouraged though. Like someone once said, "If at first you don't succeed..."

PISS ON IT!

Here's something that's totally a guy thing. Women don't need to be concerned about this issue. It has to do with the urinals. What I hate about them is the fact that everywhere I go, I seem to enter the bathroom right before the guy who always picks the middle urinal.

Tell you what I mean. I'm in a place that's not busy at all. I head to the bathroom to take a leak. Let's say the bathroom has 3 urinals and none of them are in use. Right before I'm about to enter, some other guy gets in before me and chooses the urinal in the middle. He completely disregards the ones on the ends. What the fuck is wrong with these inconsiderate pricks that they know there's someone behind them and they still do this shit? So now I have to pull my dick out less than a foot away from pisshead here, who if he had any decency would have taken one of the flanking units. Do these fuckers intentionally do that so they can get a better look at your cock? Fucking faggoty-ass bitch! Any guy who tries to look at my cock in the john will get what I call the '90 degrees'. That's when I'm in full open piss mode and I turn 90 degrees to the side so they can get a better look...while I hose them down! The other option I sometimes exercise is standing directly behind them when I come in and wait until they're pissing. Then I kick them right in the ass, shoving them forward and getting cold, pissy porcelain all over the head of their cock. Of course I explain what they did wrong so they can learn from their mistake.

Here's something that's almost as bad. When you're taking a leak and someone is doing the same beside you, why do these assholes feel the need to strike up a conversation. When my tool is in open air, there are only 2 instances in which I'm interested in conversation: 1) before I fuck and 2) immediately after I've fucked. I'm not even that comfortable talking to a close friend when we're taking a simultaneous piss. I **certainly** have no interest in talking to someone I don't know when urination is occurring. Here I am having sat for an hour and a half watching a movie, drinking what is slightly smaller than a oil drum full of Coke. Now the credits are rolling and it's time for a biological release. I get to the urinal, unzip, whip it out and start writing my name on the dry, white porcelain. Then Ballsack McGee over here gets the idea that it's the perfect time to review the film we just saw. That's great. What the fuck are we? Siskel and Ebert with our cocks out?? So I give him something to listen to. *Dude! I'm trying to take a fucking piss! My cock is in my hand and it's in the process of evacuating my bladder. Will you shut the fuck up so I can relieve myself in fucking peace??*

Some guys have no respect for others when they're at their most vulnerable.

NOSE WHAT I MEAN?

I think I may have come up with yet another Keyz-ism. Don't worry, it's not another compound profanity. The term is 'impacted snot'. The thought just crossed my mind when I was thinking about impacted teeth, and it really made sense to expand that to mucus for some reason at the time.

When your sinus are full and/or the tissue in your nose is swollen, usually from allergies, and you blow your nose only to have nothing come out, you're experiencing a case of impacted snot! The pharmacist calls it 'congestion'. Fuck that! Fuck him! If he knew anything, he'd be a real fucking doctor and not a drug peddler. Our language is complicated enough without resorting to using medical jargon in casual conversation. Tell it like it is.

If I was a pharmacist, I would change a lot of the terms around when talking to customers. I wouldn't call it 'constipation'. It would be a 'shit clog'. When a woman is on her period, she has a case of 'bloody puss'. It's a small step toward making the language less complex, but a big one.

A WILTED ROSE BY ANY OTHER NAME

This has a sort of foundation in another Carlin bit. He mentioned about how names for one generation are rarely used as commonly in the next. I think it might be time for something to actually be done about that though. I feel that people's names should have time limits. Here's an example of what I mean.

When I hear the names Cody or Dylan, I have a hard time picturing a male who has experienced puberty. The same holds true for girls' names, like Kayla and Dakota. And a lot of the names that have a sort of elementary school feel to them are these freaky, touchy-feely, natural-fiber sort of names. If I'm ever in a situation where I'm having sex with a woman named Dakota, it doesn't matter if she's old enough to be my to be my mother, I'll feel like I'm committing statutory rape! I simply can't picture any Dakota being older than 12. And if my dick is in this female, then I may as well put handcuffs on myself and wait for the authorities. Either handcuffs or a priest collar. Oh, wait. The priest collar would only be applicable if Dakota was actually a Cody.

It goes the other way as well, though. When people get to be the age that they're wearing Depends and constantly smell like Ben-Gay, it should be required that they graduate to a new name. For instance, the idea of a Lori or a Jenny sitting in a nursing home is just ludicrous to me. Sitting and watching *Wheel of Fortune* while they roll their dentures around in their mouth; it just isn't right. I'm much more comfortable with a Ruth or an Edna doing that. Or Agnes. There are plenty of names that people can graduate to.

If there is a guy sitting in the park, playing checkers, wearing a Fedora, the waist of his pants just slightly below his nipples, and he's using the name Kevin, there needs to be an intervention. Someone needs to assign him a name to fit his age. Maybe a government official can walk around with a camera and a portable ID maker, go up to these guys and inform them that they need to change their name. Arthur, Abner, Hershel, Louis, Virgil, Albert. Give him a nice list of names to choose from and make him a new ID right on the spot.

When people say the time for change is now, they aren't talking about politics or the environment. They're talking about name upgrades. Or at least they should be.

FASHION POLICE

I'm certain that I'm not the first person to notice this, but if you watch a lot of cop shows, it should be fairly obvious that cop uniforms are simply not meant for catching criminals. Have you ever worn polyester? It's the most uncomfortable shit material in the clothing market. It's pretty much the same as wearing non-waterproof plastic. Even the sound of the word 'polyester' is akin to chemistry and not clothing. Like polyethylene or polyurethane. It sounds like it should be a protectant for clothing instead of clothing itself, like ScotchGuard or some shit.

The material has no give at all either. It's like the anti-spandex. Yet at the same time, it has no strength. Well, it has more strength than a paper towel, sure. But it's nothing like jeans. Jeans aren't really all that stretchable either. If you put on a pair of tight jeans, within a few hours you'll develop deep purple lines where the material was. Right where blood should have been circulating but in fact wasn't! They aren't really meant to have give like that. Their value is in their toughness. The zippers are tough. The buttons are tough. The stitching in the ass is tough. I've been through a lot of jeans in my time. Not once have I ever had an ass blow-out in them. The bulk of them got retired to cut-offs because the legs wore through. But still, if you wear a pair of jeans for a day, then put the same pair on again the next morning, they'll feel a little looser.

Now, polyester pants on the other hand not only don't change at all in size, but are weak material when it comes to buttons, zippers and stitching. If the manufacturers had any sense at all they'd reinforce those places where the pants button. But what do you always get? Cheap plastic buttons held in place by weak thread. Why don't they use the type of fasteners that jeans use? Because if they did, it would rip right through the fucking material like it was aluminum foil. On the plus size though...oh, man. I can't believe I just wrote that. Talk about a Freudian slip! On the plus **side** though, if I was a cop, I wouldn't even need a gun. I would just push my belly out and that button would go flying at a thousand miles an hour. Probably blast a hole right through the fucking perp. Problem with that is once the button is gone, the pants would drop like a fucking bowling ball in a vacuum. Seriously, with the belt and holster and guns and fucking flashlight and everything, it would hit the ground faster than Rosie O'Donnell hits the dessert cart.

So my solution to the problem is to make cop uniforms that make sense. Jeans and leather jackets would be perfect. They're tough. They're easy to move in, provided the size is right. Follow the example of motorcycle riders. That's exactly what they wear. Sometimes they even throw on a pair of leather chaps for good measure. The last thing those guys are going to wear is fucking polyester! If they did, every time they took a spill, they'd end up with 6 pounds of gravel embedded in their flesh. I guarantee if you took one cop in jeans and leather and pitted him in a death match with another cop in polyester, the first one would win faster than you can say 'police brutality'!

It's a shame I hate authority so much or I would actually recommend a change to them. Ahh, fuck 'em! Fuck the police! Fuck, fuck, fuck the police! Yeah, fuck 'em!

BLOCK-HEADS

I'd like someone to try and explain this to me. Allow me to set the scene.

Where I work, there's a certain amount of leeway when it comes to hours of operation. Some people start at 7 AM and leave at 4. Some start at 7:30. I actually start at 8:00. The reason I do this is because we're a national company and it allows me more time to wheel and deal with people on the west coast. Ahh, who the fuck am I kidding? I do it for the extra sleep! There! Ya happy?? Anyway, when I come in, there are relatively few parking spots to pick from. Maybe a half dozen. By the time I leave at 5:00, there are never more than 4 or 5 cars left in the entire 50-ish-car lot, including mine.

So why the fuck is it that one of those few cars is always parked in the space in front of me?? Every fucking day! And it isn't like spots are assigned or anything. There's a lot of shuffling around of cars throughout any given week. Likewise it isn't the same car in front of me everyday. But I can't grasp how everyday there's *someone* parked in front of me! No matter whose car it is, that person just so happens to be working late that day!

So, you're probably asking why this is a big deal. Good question. It's because whenever I leave, it means I have to put my car in reverse to back out as opposed to just pulling through. That may sound really petty, but there's a reason I'm griping about this. Every part on every car has a finite life. Each part will only handle so many operations before it breaks.

When shifting gears, there are a large number of parts involved with the change. For me to have to take that extra step of driving in reverse, *then* driving forward, adds to the number of total shifts. It may not sound like a lot, but 5 times a week times 50 or so weeks a year: That's a lot of extra shifting! Therefore, those parts in my car will wear out quicker and die a premature death. All because some inconsiderate fuck had to park in front of me! That's bullshit. When my transmission needs to be replaced, I should file a lawsuit against all the people who parked in front of me. That's it! I'm going to start keeping a list!

If the lawsuit gets laughed out of court, which I have a feeling is very likely, I'm going to rent a Hummer. I'll park just as I normally do, but come 5 PM, if someone is in front of me, I'm not going to even bother putting it in reverse. I'm just either going to push them out of the way or, if it happens to be a smaller car, drive over the motherfucker! If I push the car, I may just go far enough to push them into a wall, then lay on the accelerator to crush the car down some! Someone drives a Lincoln Continental, I'll turn the son of a bitch into a fucking Geo before the day is out! I do that two or three days in a row and these pricks will start parking down the street before they park in front of me! Either that or just get a fucking bus pass. When it comes to driving, I'm **not** the person to piss off!

COME TOGETHER

Guys really got fucked on this one. Why is it that pussy juice is so delectable and semen is so disgusting? Going down on a woman is a fantastic experience for me. One of my favorites!

As long as the woman doesn't have brown eyes. I'll get to that in a moment. But generally speaking, feminine secretions are delicious. So why is it that the juices secreted by women should be so much more palatable than what us guys squirt. It's leverage. There's too much argument for women to be on the receiving end of oral gratification and at the same time, reject returning the favor. Another fine joke of nature.

Now then, about the brown eyes stipulation. I'm still looking for funding to do a study on vaginal juices. I've noticed that women who have red or blond hair (naturally, not artificially) and light eyes (either blue or green or some variation thereof) taste and smell infinitely better than women who have dark hair and brown eyes. This is simply from personal experience. I'm hoping to find a university or some other source to sponsor a study I would conduct. I would have 10 women with various hair and eye colors and 10 men of the same mix. The men would be blindfolded and would go down on the various women in rotation. It would essentially be a blind taste test. Kind of like Coke vs. Pepsi (bet you never thought you would read about someone likening pussy juice to cola)! The men would then rate the women's tastes on a scale of 1 to 5. It's my hypothesis that the women with light eyes and hair taste better than the women with dark hair and eyes. If that should happen to not hold true, I would be very interested to see if the men with dark hair and eyes found the taste of the dark hair/eyes girls to be better and the light hair/eyes women and men to be more compatible. I bet there would be a correlation.

If only I could get the female volunteers. Sigh.

10 MINUTES

Imagine that you have 10 minutes left to live. What would you do? Would you call your friends and family and say goodbye? Would you grab someone off the street and have really depraved sex with them? Would you run down the street naked singing show tunes? Certainly you would do something out of the ordinary.

Now keep in mind that you *will* have 10 minutes to live. You will die just like everyone else and, at some point, you'll have 10 minutes left before it happens. The funny thing is you probably won't know when that time will be. Isn't that a fucking treat?

MAKE A NAME FOR YOURSELF

It isn't quite as prevalent as it may have been in decades past, but every once in a while you'll hear someone going on about women's equality. Truthfully, I think it's a bunch of shit. Don't get me wrong! I am totally for equal treatment of women. In fact, I think women should be treated *better* than men. I don't say that so I'll get lots of pussy. I say that because I love pussy. Err...to say it another way, women got fucked over by nature (with the whole PMS thing at the very least) and I think that they should be treated better socially to make up for it. I've always said that if a woman were in charge of the country, she would improve it more in a month than any male president could do in 4 years. It's a shame that we won't get to find out until possibly 2012. Though I'm not sure Hillary would have counted as a woman (I think Bill knows a dirty little secret).

About a decade and a half ago, I worked at a repulsive chain store I refer to as RadiassCrack. This was one of those places that asked every customer who bought so much as a fuse their name, address and phone number. The place was the biggest junk mail whore on the face of the planet. So like I had done a million times before, I asked this one her name. While I couldn't possibly remember exactly what she said, it was something along the line of "Mrs. John Smith". I looked at her and asked, "Your first name is John??" knowing full well what she was going to say next. And just like my prediction she replied, in a snooty tone "No! That's my husband's name"! And it made me feel sad.

I wasn't sad because she was a cunt. If that were the case, I would have just kicked her in the ass as she walked out the door. That would have made me feel a whole lot better. What made me sad was that, in getting married, she had given up so much of her individuality that she was no longer "Ruth Smith" (or whatever the fuck the old bitch's name really was), but she was "John Smith's wife".

I'll agree that men are stupid, but after an experience like this, it's highly apparent that we don't have a corner on the market, ladies!

HAVE A SEAT

While I'm on the topic of male vs. female, it's time to clarify the rules of bathroom etiquette. The correct procedure after use of the bathroom is for the seat to be put in the *upright* position. For too long you women have been twisting things around in telling us men to put the seat down, but we aren't going for it anymore. Physical laws are now to be taken into account and a logical order shall prevail. The reasoning is as follows:

When women are in a hurry to use the can and the seat is down there's no effort involved. When the seat is up, there's actually very little effort involved in putting it down. All that needs to be done is for the seat to be flipped gently away from the tank. Because of the way the toilet seat is hinged and thanks to the earth's gravitational pull, the seat will fall neatly into place in a fraction of a second.

When men are in a hurry to use the facilities (talking about urination. For number two, the above information is equally applicable), if the toilet seat is up, there's zero effort naturally. Just unzip, pull it out and fire away. However, unlike the simplicity and negligible effort women are afforded when the seat is in the "wrong position", there's much more that needs to be taken into account. First of all, as should be apparent, gravity is now against the effort rather than in favor of, so the seat must be lifted against this natural force. And if the lid of the toilet should happen to have one of those frilly, plush, fucking foo-foo covers you women like to put on them, the strong possibility exists that the seat will not remain in the raised position. This is due to the decrease of the angle that the seat has to come to rest behind the centerline of the hinges.

While these physical hindrances are important, there's the added element of human physiology. In the woman's scenario, the front edge of the seat is in a position that's easily reachable without having to bend at the waist. In contrast, when lifting of the seat is required, unless the male happens to be a child or a midget, it's necessary for him to either bend at the waist or at the knees in order to reach the seat to raise it. Either effort puts physical pressure on the lower abdominal area. This in combination with a near-bursting bladder can make for a messy situation and a possible biohazard concern depending on the nature of the beverages consumed earlier.

Thusly, it is quite clear that it's in the best overall interest of the parties involved that the seat of the toilet be in the raised position when not in use.

Now, if you women still choose to follow the old rules, that's your prerogative. However you should be aware that us men will no longer bother putting the seat up at all and will neither be concerned with the amount of piss that splashes all over the seat. So consider the inconvenience of urine-soaked buttocks before you make your decision. Thank you.

MORE THAN A MOUTHFUL

Okay, I know that last one probably pissed the women off. Too make it up to you, I'm going to take a shot at my own: The guys.

Men are stupid. Yes, I realize you have all known this for a very long time. But this is a guy saying it. And I probably have a new reason or two you can add to your list. When it comes to food, man have a world-class degree of stupidity.

Have you ever been out with a guy and he has a bout of 'eyes-bigger-than-stomach-itis'. So at dinner, he orders a mass of food. Say you're at one of those places that has one meal that's so big, they give you a t-shirt or button or something if you finish it all. The world's biggest steak. The Mount Everest sundae. A bowl of chili so big, you can fucking bathe in it. This is like the call of the wild to men. It isn't something that the male psyche will allow to be ignored. So he orders it. When it comes, he starts off strong. Knife and fork flying at lightning speed. Halfway through, he starts to slow down, but he's still going. By the time he gets to the last bite, his eyes are glazed over and he looks like he's slipping into a coma. This rocket scientist you're sitting across from was full halfway through the meal, but even though what they brought out of the kitchen was enough food to choke a fucking elephant, he will not stop until the plate is clean. This is a genetic defect in the Y-chromosome. It's called the "stupid-as-fuck" gene. This poor stupid bastard is going to end up with stretch marks from one fucking entrée, but he's going to finish it. True, in about a half hour he'll be in the hospital because his stomach blew up, but you can't blame him. He's just a man.

While overeating to the point of gastrointestinal trauma is pretty bad, it's a distant second to men's disregard for the spice and/or heat content in food. I think this one may actually be a written rule in "The Man Book". It's apparently forbidden for a man to blow on his food to cool it down, no matter how hot it is. Perhaps it stems from the whole "blowing equals felatio" school of though. Homophobia is the cause of a lot of stupid male behavior. Let's take soup. If the soup is so fucking hot that it's melting the silverware, it's not allowed to be artificially cooled in any way. In an hour, this guy is going to be missing the roof of his mouth. Doesn't matter. No blowing on the soup. No adding ice. Just eat it.

Stupidity comes in many forms, ladies. But in all of it's glory, no woman has ever mastered it as well as a man. God help us.

POOF!

It should go without saying that I have some strange thoughts. And here's another!

I wonder how society would be different if it were customary that instead of death, people just disappeared at random. Like, we have death now. And for the most part death is scientific. It appears at some times to have a random element, but there haven't really been any unexplainable deaths. Every corpse that has been though a morgue has had a reason it was there, be it heart failure, trauma, electrocution. In every incident there was a reason the former person's respiratory and circulatory functions ceased to exist. But what if that were all taken away.

What if any person at any time could simply vanish? There were no risk factors, only randomness. What effect do you think that would have on society as a whole? How would it affect business? How would personal and family relationships be different? One minute you would be having dinner with someone and the next, they're just gone. People would have to grow accustomed to it. *"Oh, great! Now I get stuck with the check!"*

But it wouldn't all be bad. It would probably make one-night stands a lot easier to pull off.

WHAT'S THE DIFFERENCE?

I don't know if I'm getting more philosophical with age. I've noticed that I tend to think about the meaning of life more often than I used to. I guess it could be because I have more free time. Anyway...

I have most recently been thinking about the whole universe. Think about all the things that are smaller than us. Squirrels, snakes, mice, insects, bacteria, viruses. Organisms that out number us from ten times through a billion. And also think about all the things that are larger than us. Not only trees and elephants and shit, but also like moons, planets, comets, asteroids, stars, galaxies. Things that are billions of times our size. When you get down to it, we really account for very little. We are, in essence, totally insignificant.

Say you're out with a friend playing tennis. Not a real game, but just out goofing around. You hit a little yellow ball back and forth, and someone decides they want to show off and that person smacks the ball way into the air. It goes over the fence and lands in a puddle, some stagnant water just outside of the court. Standing water tends to be a breeding ground for bacteria. So now the ball, soaked with this water is covered with the bacteria that was in the water. Compared to a bacterium, a tennis ball is pretty fucking big! You could fit a whole shitload of bacteria on a tennis ball. You could probably fit six, six and a half billion bacteria on a tennis ball.

Is it not possible that we could be pretty much the same thing? That we as individuals have no more purpose than the bacteria in the water? Maybe the earth itself is just a giant tennis ball and we're simply bacteria crawling pointlessly around on it.

Maybe.

ITCH-THEOLOGY

Have you ever had one of those really persistent itches that won't go away? The kind of itch that just gets worse and worse the more you scratch it? I had one on my hand recently that I almost scratched through to the other side.

Shortly after that I thought of a foolproof solution. The great part about it is that it doesn't require any scratching at all. The next time you get a really bad itch, go into the kitchen and take out a meat-tenderizing mallet then hit the itch with it repeatedly. At some point the affected area will go numb, thus no longer itching. Problem solved.

A.I. (ANIMAL INTELLIGENCE) - PART 2

I've said before that animals have it all figured out. Think of what a tomcat does. When he's horny, he finds a girl cat in heat, jumps right on and goes to town. None of this fucking courting. No bringing roses and taking her to an expensive restaurant. None of that 'meeting the parents' shit. And if the girl cat gets pregnant, he doesn't need to have anything to do with it. No paying child support. No need to appear on Maury Povich, talking about which cat is whose "baby daddy". He just goes right on to the next chick.

Hell, the domestic animals are so clever that they have even figured out how to get an entirely different species to take care of them for nothing in return. Food, water, shelter, health care. Everything, and the animal doesn't have to do Jack Shit for it. Well, maybe bestow a little affection just to keep things running smoothly. But that animal doesn't have to go out and find a job so they're bringing home a contribution. They take a shit and have someone there to clean it up. What a fucking grift!

THE WONDERS OF TECHNOLOGY

I'm pretty sure that most of the people who are reading this book probably don't listen to public radio. Though, few people have gone through childhood steering altogether clear of public television, so everyone should catch my drift on this one.

Here's something that will be a major technological breakthrough: a television or radio that can detect and mute not only commercials, but also efforts during pledge drives. How many of you remember watching Sesame Street and having a good time with Big Bird and Cookie, doing sing-alongs, learning (well, you didn't know you were learning, but you didn't really give a shit). Then three minutes into the show, some asshole comes on babbling about how public television relies on viewer support and how you can keep the programming on the air if you send them money. And what they were asking was fucking ridiculous. 80 dollars for a cheap ass umbrella and a tote bag?? What are they, out of their fucking minds?? For Christ's sake, put Grover back on! He was gonna teach me to count to 10 in Spanish, douchebag!

For those who have never heard it, public radio is the same way. I can't wait until they have radios that can detect when these pledge drives are going on and, when some jackoff comes on looking for donations, mutes itself. Or better yet, turns to another station until the music resumes. We need to get Sony on that project.

DON'T BE SO HARD-ON ME!

There are about a dozen remedies for erectile dysfunction nowadays. No matter the brand, they all come with the same warning. If you experience priapism, an erection lasting more than four hours, consult a physician immediately.

If I ever get an erection for more than four hours, I'm going to fuck **everything!** At least until it goes away. And it will save me a co-pay.

THOUGHTS THAT ARE TOO SHORT FOR THEIR OWN SECTIONS IN THIS BOOK EVEN THOUGH THE TITLE IS ALMOST A PARAGRAPH ITSELF

- Today's children are tomorrow's assholes. And in many cases, the transition has already begun.

- New advertising campaign: Fords are for Bertos. If you don't understand that, you need to listen to the show more.
- If you're ever stuck for an insult, try calling the person "ball mange"! The thought alone may be enough to turn them green.
- It pains me to say that the French actually did something right. They made 'yes' (oui) easy to type with one hand. All three letters are right next to each other.
- Stupid cliché: Cute as a button. I have lots of shirts with several buttons on them and not a single one of them is particularly cute.
- You know a word that sounds 100% appropriate for what it describes? Sludge. It just sounds so right. I like when words do that.
- There's an after-market car-customizing company called OBX Racing Sports. I question their name selection. Doesn't OBX sound like a tampon designed for women who skate and snowboard and such?
- Another company name on a truck I saw: Belfor National Disaster Team. What's a Belfor? For ringing, silly! I know. Just horrible.
- Here's a song lyric that always bothered me: "Get up, Get up, Get up, Get down on it"! Make up your fucking mind, will you?!?
- What's the singular for 'rice'? Would it be a 'rie'? Rice doesn't always exist in spoonfuls. Sometimes there's just one lone grain on the floor. What would you call it?
- Here's something I can't stand: Old people who whistle or hum. Christ! Are the elderly so uncomfortable

with ambient sound that they need to constantly produce their own noise! Get in the fucking box, old man!
- Does anyone else remember when people used the word "beefed" for 'farted'? *Who beefed in here?!?* Whatever happened to that?
- A depressing thought: eventually, probably in the near future, you'll run out of soap and have to buy some more. Sigh.
- 2 of the ingredients in some Ambrosia Salad recipes are bananas and mayonnaise. Who the fuck eats this shit?!?

HOW NOW, EYEBROW?

Whenever I hear people try to describe the humor of The Awful Show, it's somewhat common to hear it referred to as being "lowbrow". I'm pretty cool with that. I take a degree of pride in being that way myself. But what the hell does it mean??

Where does terminology like that come from? Was it that at some time there was this guy with the bizarre birth defect of having his eyebrows under his eyes who went around telling dirty jokes? Or it just could be the opposite of "highbrow". Because I can understand where highbrow comes from. You've got all the hoity-toity stuck-up cunts and faggots who think they're "high society" and think they're so superior to everyone else. Whenever I see someone like that, I walk up to them, pull my dick out and wipe it on them. They get this really shocked look on their face and their eyebrows go up. So I can understand that term.

FRIVOLITY IN THE FRIENDLY SKIES

There was some time ago where my job required me to go to trade shows and shit. A note about me: I don't like to travel. It isn't that I'm afraid of flying or anything. I just simply don't give a shit about any region beyond that in which I live and work. I don't care about how a little cum-trickle of a river created the deepest, widest canyon in the country. I couldn't give a flying fuck about a giant concrete and steel phallus that employs 400,000 people and reaches 3,000 stories into the sky. I don't give a shit about pyramids, coliseums, catacombs, big fucking walls, or some mausoleum in India that looks like a giant engorged clit. I don't...fucking...care!

Anyway, I had to make a trip to New Orleans once (this was before it turned into Atlantis). On the airplane ticket, it said that a meal would be included. For the duration of the flight, no meal was ever brought to me. And I don't count the little box with the apple and the Sun Chips. That's not a fucking meal. When I was young and sat down for dinner, my mother never put a piece of fruit and a small bag of chips on a plate and said "Dinner is served". Since the airline didn't live up to their obligation, I can't help but wonder how far I could have taken it. Could I have demanded that the stewardesses collect in the little kitchenette area and cook me a meal? And if they didn't I would sue them. In this country, I don't have a doubt in my mind that I could have done that. I could have taken them to court and sued them for $20 for not giving me a meal and $10,000,000 in punitive damages. And you know what? I would have won. I guarantee it.

And please take note of how I use the term stewardess. I

don't call them flight attendants. If all they're doing is bringing me drinks and pillows, they're stewardesses. Whenever they're willing to unzip my pants and take my penis into their throat repeatedly, fine, then they can be *'flight attendants'*.

FUCK CHILDREN!

No, this has nothing to do with pedophilia. I don't mean it literally, ya fruitcakes!

I'm talking about these fucking school buses. The fucking nerve of the people who make the legislation regarding the equipping of these buses with little stop signs that pop out whenever they stop to pick up or drop off these little bastards.

I don't see any other vehicles with these safety measures. What about regular buses, the ones adults who have jobs use. The buses for people who are actually making a contribution to the gross national product. Hell, no! But the ones that carry these little twat droppings, who are contributing nothing to society. That are, in fact, leeching off of hard working property owners by going to public schools, they get protected like they're an endangered fucking species! Have you looked around lately? Do you notice any shortage of children on this planet?

Fuck that shit! From now on, when I see a flashing stop sign swing out from the side of a bus, I'm considering it a notice, not a warning, that kids are nearby. And that means open season on these little fucks. It's time to go bumper hunting! I want to see Social Studies books flying through the air, splattered with blood! I want to see a Barbie lunch box with a femur sticking out of it!

That would teach these self-righteous pricks to put children ahead of adults on the ladder of importance!

STICK IT!

I'd like to come out with a line of involuntary bumper stickers. Here's an example of what I have in mind.

You can't take a 5-minute drive anymore without seeing those fucking fish symbols on the back of some of these cocksuckers' cars. I think we need a bumper sticker that we can put over these ridiculous things that says "KEEP YOUR FUCKING RELIGION TO YOURSELF, DOUCHEBAG"!! Or another appropriate sticker would be one that says "NO ONE GIVES A FUCK IF YOUR BASTARD KID IS ON THE HONOR ROLL"!!

Or maybe go a slightly different route with a sticker you can use on various car brands. For instance, when you come across a Ford of any kind, you'll be ready to put a sticker on that says "DON'T LAUGH! IT'S ALL I COULD AF*FORD*!" and make the 'ford' part of 'afford' the actual logo.

At this point in the book, maybe you've noticed my loathing of Fords. I want to take a moment to explain why. I've noticed that these vehicles have a mythical power not understood by man nor being explainable by standard scientific methods. Fords have the ability, much more than any other make of car, to turn the person behind the steering wheel into a complete and total fucking asshole! I've know people who own Fords. Some of them are the sweetest, kindest people you could ever meet. But when they get behind the wheel of their Escort or F-150, watch the fuck out!! They become the most hazardous thing on the pavement! But even in addition to that, I've known Fords to be the most faulty, high-maintenance vehicles going. You may be familiar with the use of Ford as an acronym. 'Found On Road Dead' is an excellent translation. A more popular one is "Fixed Or Repaired Daily", though I must admit I don't like that one. It's lazier than the prior one. 'Fixed' and 'repaired' have the same meaning. So while I appreciate the sentiment, it isn't my favorite. My favorite is one I came up with myself. And it draws attention to the former issue I have with Fords. To me, Ford stands for "For Obviously Retarded Drivers". That just has a comfortable feel to it for me.

Before I get back to my point of this segment (which it appears I have strayed **way** far from), I'll say that I'm a Dodge driver. And like Ford, one must question if Dodge is an acronym too. I would like point out that it in fact is not. It is, however, a descriptive term. 'Dodge' is what the subject vehicle has to do to get around all the fucking broken-down Fords cluttering up the road! That's pretty much just common sense, but every once in a while it bears expressing.

Back to my main point, I would like to clarify that just because these custom-made involuntary stickers aren't in mass production yet doesn't mean that some existing stickers wouldn't work just fine. Like when you're walking through the parking lot, make sure you keep a handful of Hillary Clinton stickers that can easily be placed over top of any Obama stickers you might encounter. Feel free to update this concept for future elections.

Aside from the whole vandalizing element, I would actually like to see someone produce some *oversized* bumper stickers. Even for sheer novelty purposes. Like those big ass sunglasses you can win at a carnival. The ones that are 3 times wider than any human's head. They're making everything bigger nowadays, so why not follow suit. Like those jumbo double-wide trucks that look like they've got big fat hips. The trucks that apparently draw the eye of incompetent redneck hillbilly fucks who don't have the intelligence to park the thing in a single space. Actually, those would be perfectly appropriate to don said stickers.

But I want to be clear that when I say oversized, I mean motherfucking **oversized**!! Not like 50% or 75% bigger than the average sticker. I'm talking about stickers that take up the whole fucking back end of the car! A foot and a half tall and six foot wide! Minimum! You want to advertise a thought or a belief, then get some fucking balls and do it right!

But of course bumper stickers are not as much in vogue as they were in decades past. The big thing now seems to be those translucent decals that go across the back windows of trucks. I'll admit those are somewhat cool, but the subject matter is all wrong. Every time I see one, it's portraying something like Jesus. Or maybe more often, the American flag, either by itself or with an eagle in front of it. To me, that's boring. If you're going to put something like that on your vehicle, then do it right. I want to see a truck whose back window is covered with a picture of a giant vagina on it! You could do it with either the vagina in the middle with the two legs spreading out toward the doors or, if you wanted to get serious, have the vagina be sideways so it takes up the whole window! That would be fucking great! The clit would look like a fucking pink basketball! Though, the other way wouldn't be too bad either! Can you imagine being behind a truck with one of the spread leg versions and all of a sudden that little window in the middle opens up. Hah! Jesus! I'd have to pull over and take public transportation until I could stop laughing.

RAPE ME, MY FRIEND

Okay, it's time to clear this up once and for all. There is no such thing as date rape. And I don't mean that a woman can't be raped on a date. That isn't what I'm talking about. That's just plain rape. I'm talking about these situations that women get themselves in where they get all drunk and fucking drugged up and shit, sleep with a guy, then cry foul in the morning because the guy took advantage of the situation. How can that even be considered something as brutal and sadistic as rape??

First of all, if you women would expect any behavior of a man other than taking advantage of you when you're fucked up, then you're pathetically and painfully stupid! Have you never been with a man before?? Are you completely oblivious to the fact that at any given time during a date the thought on a man's mind is probably "Man, I hope I get to stick my cock in her later"?? Get fucking lucid, ladies! And even if you can't wrap your minds around this notion, then at least have the presence of mind to know that if you can't handle your buzz, then you have no business getting drunk or high in the first fucking place!

To be perfectly fair, if you women are going to run with the whole battle cry that No means No!, then we guys are going to counter that with Yes means Fucking YES!! End of story!

BLACK SHEEP

Remember the movie "Babe"? In order to get the sheep to do what the little pig wanted, he had to give them the secret phrase "Baa-Ram-Ewe". Am I the only one who thinks this is a blatant reference to sodomy??

Let's break it down. The first word is "Baa". This is clearly the first phonetic of the word "Butt". The next one is "Ram". You don't need to be a porn director to know what this is referring to. Then the last one "Ewe" is just a differently spelled version of the word "you". So the phrase comes down to "Butt Ram You" or to put it another way "Fuck you in the ass"!

And I thought that was supposed to be a kids' movie. Though this does explain why you always hear about farmers getting sheep up the ass. The sheep apparently like it!

SHOW SOME BALLS!

Toy marbles first went into mass production in the 1870s, and I think it's safe to say that the market has gradually slowed throughout those years. As such, I would like to offer a word of advice to those marble manufactures out there who are feeling the crunch.

I think you should keep producing the same marbles you always have, but start calling them *Fucking Shit Balls*. With a name that dirty, kids would have a whole new interest in them. Sales would skyrocket. Enjoy the boom.

POETRY FOR THE DISEASED

I would like to take a moment if I may and quote a *Sons of Butchers* song.

Fuck the shit.
Fuck the fucking shit fuck.
Shit the fuck.
Shit the shitting fuck shit.

Never has anyone in the history of music; not Puccini, not Wagner, not Rossini, not even Mozart! Never has there been an artist who has written anything so eloquent as these simple words.

</sarcasm>

GREEN LIGHT, RED LIGHT

One good thing about running a red light: The asshole behind you usually won't follow you. Then you just have to worry about the asshole in front of you.

On the other side of that, something I would like to see civil engineers start designing into roads are 6-inch thick metal plates that shoot up out of the ground the moment the light turns red. This would do one of two things to the offending drivers. If it popped up in front of them, they'd slam right into it and go flying through the windshield. Or if they were over top of it when it shot up, it would toss the ass-end of the car over the front, putting the prick on his roof.

Either way, it would give a whole new fucking meaning to those yellow lights!

YOU WOULDN'T LIKE ME WHEN I'M ANGRY.

In 2008, they came out with the movie "The Incredible Hulk". It featured the fine actor Edward Norton, the ultra-sexy Liv Tyler (Her mother must have been a goddess to offset Steve Tyler's hideous genes), and the comical and talented Tim Roth. It got rave reviews from numerous critics and publications. Despite all of this, I still don't count it as a legitimate movie.

With fresh cutting edge cinema technology, the late 80s began the rebirth of comic book movies. As of this writing, they have enjoyed nearly 2 decades of popularity and the genre still shows no sign of waning. But there was one simple unwritten rule to this rebirth: You get one shot. You can make as many sequels as you like, but you can't revive the same comic character twice. *The Incredible Hulk* broke that rule. In 2003, the movie "The Hulk" was written by Stan Lee (the creator of the comic) and Jack Kirby. In charge of direction, they put Ang Lee. I know, "Who the fuck is that?" was my response too. Here's a guy who has directed a total of 4 American movies (not counting the ones that were eventually remade from their Japanese counterparts). Not a single one of these was spectacular in any way, shape, or form. The end result: one of the shittiest revivals to ever curse the screen.

Now fast forward 5 years. Out comes *The Incredible Hulk*. It's infinitely better than the first attempt. But the fact remains that **it is too fucking late**!! You only get one shot! There are no "do-overs" in Hollywood. And I don't give a flying rat fuck about "Well, the other remake was from the comic and this one is from the TV show". No, bullshit! It's the same fucking character. You had one shot, and you fucked it up. End of discussion.

You want to remake something? How about giving "KISS Meets the Phantom of the Park" a shot. Trust me. That would be a lot harder to fuck up considering the original!

DO PAMPERS COME IN THONGS?

I realize that this whole thing is not part of any snack I did and it was actually a discussion we had in one of the shows. I don't particularly care about that. Ever since that discussion had aired, I've taken a lot of shit for what I feel was actually a noble act on my part. Let me start at the beginning for those of you that may not have heard the story.

When I was in high school, I was a nerd extraordinaire. And this was quite a bit before it was cool to be a geek. I had a very difficult time getting dates. Even the few decent looking girls I saw caught wind of my geekdom and ran the other way. So I took just about any girl I could get. One time I hung out with a girl who had MS. She had a difficult time walking but she was a sweet girl so I approached her and asked her out. She accepted and was in amazement that anyone would want to go out with her. We had seen each other a couple times before I met her mother. Like the girl, the mother was very sweet. She had taken me aside once and actually thanked me for asking her daughter out. She had said that the doctors don't expect her to live very much longer and she was just thrilled she could experience dating before she passed. That made me feel very good about myself. The next time I saw her, I asked if she felt like fooling around (no one should die without ever knowing at least what it's like to get felt up). She had no objections. So here we are cuddling and I have my hand under her shirt and she's moaning and getting all excited so I allow my hand to head down to her genitals...

Before I finish the story, there's one thing that I hadn't said about her. It's not uncommon at all for people with MS to have incontinence issues. She happened to be one of those people.

So my hand goes between her legs and I feel that under her clothes, she has a diaper. You can call them protective undergarments if it makes you feel less dirty as you read this, but I prefer to call things as they are and not disguise words under jargon. While I was thrown by what I felt, I didn't let it deter me as it was making her feel good. I just kept going and tried not to think about it. It was bad enough the girl had this crippling ailment. I wasn't about to make her feel worse by freaking out because she couldn't control her bladder so well.

The bottom line of the story: I felt up a girl who wore a diaper. If you want to call me a sick, twisted fuck for that, go right ahead. It wouldn't be the first time I've heard it. But at least realize why I did it and give me a little credit for doing something nice for another person when no one else would.

My whole reason for rehashing this is to point out that there are a lot of sicker people out in the world than I. Do a Google search for "forced infancy". You'll come up with about half a billion porn sites based on getting sexual pleasure from seeing grown women in diapers. I, in contrast to those type of people, did not get turned on by the girl having a diaper. It just happened to be there. So quit making me out to be some kind of sexual deviant when there's so much worse. If you want to call me a deviant for being turned on by spandex, fine. Go right ahead. I am a proud spandexophile! But don't nail me to the cross for this.

And if you still think I'm a sick fuck, eat a turd. With walnuts and chocolate syrup, you pricks!

MICRO$HIT

Say what you will about Micro$oft; you can't deny they're brilliant in their practices. Unethical and evil...but brilliant nonetheless. I'm convinced that they knew exactly what they were doing when they released Vista. Yes, it's just about the worst operating system since Windows Me. But do you honestly think such an enormous conglomerate would release such a horrible product by accident? I don't. I think the entire thing was staged.

For those of you who were around in the 80s, try to remember the release of the 'new Coke'. If you can't recall, in 1985, Coca-Cola released what they simply called at the time "*the new taste of Coca-Cola*". It was meant to be a sweeter cola than the original. While it didn't taste **bad** necessarily, it was piss in comparison to the original formula. Then after a while, they returned to the original formula under the name *Coca-Cola Classic*. Sales went through the roof.

Micro$oft was apparently paying attention to this trend and pulled the same scam. They released Vista on every new computer sold at larger retailers. In fact I'm not so sure you could even go to a Best Buy or Walmart or any retailer and buy a new computer that didn't come with Vista loaded, at least until Windows 7 came out. Why? #1 - So Micro$oft could sell a shitload more copies of Windows XP, the clearly superior of the two operating systems, and #2 – to make the following OS, Windows 7, look good no matter how badly it sucked. Not too bad, Billy. You certainly did your homework.

OH-OH-OH-OH, WHAT A WRETCHED FEELING!

It should be clear by this point in the book that I loathe Toyota, even worse than Ford! I would love nothing more than for them to be caught in unfair business practices, get sued for billions of dollars and go bankrupt. And have all the officers of the company die in a fire. But that would just be a bonus.

In the first quarter of 2008, it was reported that Toyota had passed General Motors in US sales. I have no allegiance to GM, but this completely turned my stomach. However, it did further my theory that the general American public is fucking stupid and that they have no loyalty. And I'm not talking about the Americans reading this book. I'm talking about the other Americans. Unless you happen to be reading this book **and** own a Toyota, in which case, I hope you get an open sore on your anus!

In this day and age of global terrorism and war, it shouldn't be difficult to find a little loyalty in the American public. But here you have the majority of sales going to a Japanese company over an American manufacturer. And I know what all the Toyota bitches out there are saying. *Well, Toyotas are assembled in the United States and Toyota employs American workers.* Fuck that shit. Ever heard of a little thing called outsourcing? There are a lot of American companies that employ people 12,000 miles away in different countries. Doesn't mean that they cease to be an American company though! It's all about whose pocket the majority of the profits go into and who is in charge. If the CEO has slanted eyes and doesn't reside in North America, they're a foreign company as far as I'm concerned. And as far as the American plants go, the people who work there don't work there because it's owned by Toyota. They work there because...well, because there's *work there*! Those plants could be owned by General Motors or Chrysler or, as much as it hurts to say it, Ford. It isn't like GM would buy the plant and people would quit because it wasn't owned by Toyota anymore!

If you would, try to remember your history lessons. Back in the 30s and 40s there was a little conflict called World War

II. You know? And in that war, two of the parties involved were the American and the Japanese? **And** they were on different sides killing each other? Is that ringing any bells? Did America somehow forget that these fuckers were the enemy? Does the name "*Pearl Harbor*" jog anyone's memory?

So for you Toyota whores out there. Try and show a little fucking loyalty to the country you live in. Buy an American car, fuckers!

And as a post script to this, yes, I'm aware that many of the parts of American cars are foreign, but don't let that deter you. Zen Buddhists have a saying: The food is not the lunch. Well, the *parts* are not the *car*.

EMOTI-PHONE

Here's another technological idea I had. Have you ever talked to your significant other on your phone and gotten into a fight and one or the other hangs up? Then one of you calls the other one back (to either fight more or make up, depending on how long you have been together), but the other person doesn't pick up the phone and it goes to voice mail? Don't you get a weird feeling when the machine answers and their voice is completely different than it was when you just spoke to them because of the emotions involved? I hate that.

So my idea is for phone manufacturers to install an "emo-circuit" that can detect how the person was feeling when they last used the phone, and adjust the voicemail accordingly. This can either be done by adjusting the regular voicemail digitally or the person can have several different messages for different situations. I think it would be cool for the phone to detect the user's feelings and automatically switch from "(in a bubbly tone) Hi! This is Marie! I can't come to the phone right now..." to "(sobbing) This is Marie. I'm too upset to answer the phone right now because of my cocksucker of a boyfriend...". Of course you could find a way to incorporate the caller ID as well. "(viciously) Hey, you asshole! If you can't tell I'm major fucking pissed and I have no interest in talking to you right now, and possibly ever again. I hope you fucking die..."!

I'll have to see if I can sell that idea to Apple for their next generation of iPhones.

CARS OF PREY

This is one of my more bizarre thoughts. When a Mercury Cougar crashes into a Volkswagen Rabbit, why is the damage fairly equal? If the names of these cars matched the damage the respective animals would do in nature, the situation would be a lot different. The Cougar might have a tiny scratch or two and nothing would be left of the Rabbit except maybe the chassis. They should really rethink the names of these cars. I would be inclined to rename the Hummer models after various elephants. Likewise, I would change the name of subcompacts to Groundhog or Chipmunk, depending on its speed.

And for the record, I would be sure to try to track down a Dodge Badger or a Chevy Wolverine for myself. Something little, but brutal!

And, if I may shift gears here for a moment (no pun intended), hopefully it will be a car that has one of those semi-automatic transmissions. I love my Dodge, but one thing I'm sick of is my car deciding when it wants to shift. I think Volkswagen makes some cars that allow you to shift just by pushing a button. And people are probably going to say well, why don't you just get a standard? One simple reason: If I'm driving a standard and I'm at a dead stop facing uphill, I may as well put the emergency brake on and stick up a "for sale" sign. I can't work a clutch worth a shit. If I could, with the present gas prices, I would probably be driving a motorcycle. But, like I say, I don't like the car deciding when it wants to go up or down a gear. It never fails that I'm going up a good size hill and the car thinks it doesn't have enough power to climb it in fourth, so it downshifts and the tachometer jumps to 8,000. I hate that shit. That was off-topic, but fuck it! I needed to fit that in somewhere.

BASIC MATH

Here's another vehicle thing that bothers me. When you see an off-road vehicle that has "4x4" written on it somewhere, does it not sound like it should have 16 wheels? I've never seen a 16-wheel vehicle. I've heard of an 18-wheeler, but that's about as close to it as I can find. Even if it said "4+4" that would be 8 wheels. Every car or truck I've seen with this on it has had only 4 wheels total. Wouldn't it make more sense to put "2x2" on these fucking things?

YOU BET YOUR ASS

Here's another sign of true stupidity in the United States. And I'm sure other countries, too. Gambling venues. Vegas, Atlantic City, Reno. All these places with these multi-million, even billion-dollar casinos that are constantly taking in money by the truckloads. Do people not realize that in every case, the deck (no pun intended again) is stacked against them? Are they that fucking naïve to think that they're going to walk into a casino and leave with more money than they walked in with? Or even walk out with anything close to the same amount? Anyone who does belongs in a fucking asylum, heavily medicated. And for those that don't, why the fuck do they still go to these places? You know why? Because they're fucking stupid!

And if you go to these places because you like the games, do yourself a favor and download them or go to a software store and purchase a software pack called "Hoyle Casino". The latest release has 16 different games in it. You don't even have to move out of your chair. Hell, you can even play the games butt naked! Why go to some place that's crowded with drunken smokers 2,000 miles away from home just to play a game?

If intelligence ever became a dominant trait in humans, casinos would cease to exist. However, judging by the present output of public schools, I think they'll be safe for a long time.

THE POWER OF DICE COMPELS YOU!

Sometimes I have to wonder if I become temporarily possessed by Andrew Dice Clay. Some of the things that come out of my mouth almost convince me of it. Example: I was driving home from work and here's this jackoff driving slowly in the left hand lane. So I speed up, pass him on the right, cut him off, flip him the bird and out of my mouth, with no kind of forethought at all, comes "Get outta the way, shitwank!"

And I chuckle to myself. Shitwank? What the fuck is that?? Is that someone who likes to masturbate feces? It's a sick world. If there are guys in Milwaukee keeping the heads of Cambodian teenagers in their fridge, who knows? There are probably some loonies out there jerking off turds!

I have to laugh, though. The only other option is to be afraid. When my head goes around and I spit pea soup, then I'll reevaluate.

KEEP YOUR WINGS CLOSED!

Government is all about overpopulation. They have to be. It isn't blatantly obvious, but there are a number of discrete policies and occurrences that when examined closely practically spell it out.

For example, and this isn't referring to humans precisely. But look at how the government handles endangered species. When it's discovered that the population of a species of animal is dwindling or dying out, what do they do? They create laws making the hunting of that animal illegal. They'll take away whatever human rights they deem necessary (the government has never had a problem taking rights away) in order to keep that species from going extinct. Yet, if there's an overabundance of animals, like pigeons, they won't lift a finger to help thin them out. To me, that's a classic double standard. Here you have these filthy, flying disease bags, shitting all over anything under the sun in swarms, yet legislation encouraging people to kill them is never passed. No special tax breaks for licensed pigeon exterminators. Not a fucking thing.

I hope one day for all the pigeons in the country to flock to Washington, DC, and cover the entire area with a thin coating of shit. So much so that no one in the area can touch anything that isn't covered with white, runny fecal matter. And all of the politicians breathe in the dust from it and become deathly ill. Then maybe they'll get off their fat asses and solve the issue.

THE RETAIL CESSPOOL

Have you ever been in one of those big stores that charge more for their merchandise than any human should ever have to pay? Wait. That's pretty vague. In fact, that describes *every* store. I'm talking about one of the big chain stores that they use as hubs or end caps for malls. J.C. Penney, Macy's, Neiman Marcus. Or if you're a little older, Gimble's or Lazarus. The kind of stores that have the cash registers in little islands throughout the store instead of at the exit like a normal fucking business.

When you go shopping, at a place like that, have you noticed that more often than not, there are never any clerks at the cash registers? And you have to go searching for them just so you can purchase 2 pairs of jeans and a garden hose?

You know what I say? Fuck that shit! Just take the stuff and walk out the fucking door. Any store that requires me to walk around and find a clerk to buy shit deserves to get merchandise boosted! And if you happen to be buying clothes that have those little security ink grenades attached, fuck 'em! Let them blow up. I guarantee if enough people start doing this, it will become a fashion trend. Shit, look at tie dye!

DOES INSURANCE COVER STUPIDITY?

On my way to work last week I saw a guy driving a Toyota. I noticed that something just wasn't quite right about it though. After looking for a few moments, I noticed that the symbol was upside down. And I have a really hard time believing that it was like that by mistake. Unless he has a retiree from the Special Olympics as his body shop guy, that thing is like that on purpose.

But what possible purpose could doing that serve? To prove that the owner of the car is a douche? Well, it certainly does that, but I doubt that's the driver's intention. Maybe it's because the upside-down "T" looks like an erect cock and balls. Why would anyone want that on their car anywhere though?? Why not just go and get a vanity license plate that reads "I SUK COK". That would be a much clearer message anyway.

This is an example of what I like to refer to as "self vandalism". The act of making one's car look ridiculous in an effort to make people think the driver is cool. I would like to make it known to anyone who is reading this that the actual effect of such actions is exactly the opposite. It does nothing more than prove you're a complete and total fucking loser.

There are plenty of forms of this type of crime. And I'm not referring to those who drive some piece of shit because it's all they can afford. If some guy who drives an '85 Toyota that is more rust and primer paint than it is metal wants to scratch out the "OTA" from the back so it just reads "TOY", I don't have a problem with that. As far as I'm concerned, anything you can do to that type of "vehicle" that detracts from the fact that it shouldn't even be on the road is fine by me. After all, we can't all drive Bentleys and Aston Martins.

What I'm talking about are thing like spinning rims. What the fuck are you trying to prove with those fucking things?? Are you trying to fool those of us without those retarded modifications into thinking that the wheels are still moving when they're actually not? Are we supposed to stand there in disbelief saying "Hey! How did he do that? His car isn't moving, but his wheels are! Wow! This must be the coolest guy in the world!" Guess what, shithead? No one with an IQ above their shoe size is going to say that. In fact, the actual response will be more like "Those are the stupidest fucking things I've ever seen"!

Spoilers are another felony of car fashion I have no tolerance for. And I wish to leave out spoilers that are a standard part of the car. It has gotten to the point that if you want to drive a certain make and model of car, there's the possibility that the car manufacturer doesn't produce that particular car without a spoiler. So in a case like that, I'll offer a degree of leniency. But the ones I will not are the ones that are third party modifications. Like the ones that are a different color than the car and stick up higher than the fucking roof!

Allow me to explain a little bit of physics to the spoiler jack-off crowd. The purpose of a spoiler is to provide an increase in traction by increasing downforce on the back end of the car when going at high speeds. This is done by harnessing the passing wind, much like the wing of a plane. Now for some harsh reality. #1 – your little piece of shit coupe doesn't go fast enough to be able to utilize the effects of a spoiler. You may think your car can go 200 mph, but the only way that will ever happen is if you drive it off a cliff. A car in free fall can quite often achieve that speed. Otherwise, fucking forget it! #2 – a spoiler only works when the wing is set up at an angle. Every spoiler I've seen is flat. Totally parallel to the ground. This does nothing to increase downforce, and can quite often help to lift the back end off the ground. If you're hoping to take the car up on the front two wheels, then the flat wing will have a lot better chance of doing that than in serving its intended purpose.

All of these car modifications only serve one purpose: to prove to onlookers that the driver has insufficient genitalia. And I phrase it that way on purpose because there are times when women are the drivers of said vehicles. Guys with a four-inch pencil dick who perpetually suffers from premature ejaculation, and whores who had a kid when they were 16 and have a vagina reminiscent of a windsock, both in tension and size. If you fall under either of these categories, feel free to let everyone know by modding your ride. Happy driving, fuckheads!

WHO PISSED IN THE GENE POOL?

Euthanasia shouldn't be just for the terminally ill or vegetative. The choice of living or not living should be focused on the quality of life, not the inevitability of death. I would like to see euthanasia clinics take the same path as family planning clinics. When a guy thinks his life sucks, he goes in for a counseling session. If death seems to be in the guy's best interest, they hook him up to the Kevorkian-5 (or whatever they choose to call a machine that gives lethal injections) and away he goes.

So now that we have the means, we need to come up with a methodology of who is a candidate for euthanasia. I would go with the principle that any one who is unappealing, for one reason or another, to the gender of their sexual preference can be exterminated. Anyone who has an exceedingly difficult time getting laid (without paying for it) can take the needle. This would include anyone who is crippled, fat, retarded, diseased, or just plain ugly. We can also throw those unfortunates with bladder or bowel control problems. No one wants to be doing someone and end up with a bed full of shit or piss. At least when it isn't a fetish. And don't bother mentioning the girl with MS. She's already dead. Feel better?

That takes care of the voluntary people, but I think that the whole idea needs to be expanded to involuntary extermination for people who are a general annoyance to those around them. People who drive rudely (you knew I had to start with that one), anyone who has a really annoying laugh, anyone with psychological problems (I'm looking at all you OCD fuckers), people with B.O. who go out in public smelling like a bucket full of rancid Ritz crackers and shit, line them all up! Let's add those with permanent STDs like herpes. Can you believe these commercials that show a couple in which one person has herpes and the other one doesn't?? Anyone who would be hooking up with someone who has herpes, no matter how safe they're being, deserves to get it. So put both of them in the line! There are an abundance of other categories of people that can be added to this list, so feel free to add your own.

Lastly, I know there'll naturally be a lot of shitheads...pardon me...religious people who will be up at arms about killing humans. Rest assured, when ever they show up at the clinics, they'll go to the head of the line.

IN MY PANTS

Have you ever heard a guy, usually a celebrity or politician, say "I put my pants on one leg at a time like everyone else". I've tried this. Here's an experiment next time you're getting dressed. Take your pants, put in one leg and pull them all the way up. Now, put the other leg in. You can't do it! Unless you're a professional contortionist, or an octopus, it's physically impossible to put pants on one leg at a time. In fact it's pretty strenuous to even have the pants up past the first knee and get the other leg in. If people mean that they put one foot in then the other, then they need to say that. But anyone who is trying to put one leg in at a time is liable to hurt themselves.

STAY INSIDE THE LINES

I like to carry an acetylene torch in my car. One reason really. When I see people who park inconsiderately, I like to help them learn a lesson. Any part of the car that's hanging over into another space gets cut off. Usually this is something as simple as a rear view mirror. Other times it's the full length of the car. I make sure I have extra time for just such occasions. As well as packing a lunch.

I'M NOT TALKING ABOUT TIM

Anyone who does any interstate driving might have noticed this. There's a heavy hauling company called Con-Way, hyphenated just like that. Doesn't that convey the impression that the trucks are driven by former criminals?

I don't know about anyone else, but I'm just a little uncomfortable with the notion that the 12-ton vehicle going 70 miles an hour just about 3 feet away from me is being driven by someone who was just released after serving time for committing a triple homicide. Maybe it's just me.

SERVING TIME

I, as yet, have not heard a legitimate argument for the use of "daylight savings time". To me, I think it's just another effort by the government to show us that they can fuck with us any time they feel like it. I think that the only reason they keep telling us to change our clocks forward and backward is to confuse us so they can keep slipping more and more taxes in and taking away more and more freedoms from our already meager lives.

One of the problems is the fact that it has gone on for so long, people just accept it like it's nothing. Think about this though. There's only one time: right now. The past isn't time anymore and the future isn't time yet. The only time we have is now. I can understand the whole earth being split up into time zones. I'm cool with that. It would be pretty fucked up to look outside at noon on one side of the planet and see the sun then travel to the other side of the planet later on, look out at 'noon' and see darkness. So having an hour increase or decrease every 15 planetary degrees is fine. But here's the issue I have. There can only be *one time*. Here's an example.

When I first wrote this notion down in the summer, the clock on my PC said 3:44 PM. Six months later to the minute, the clocks had been changed and that meant at that moment 24 hours times approximately 182 days later, my PC clock read 2:44 PM. Where the fuck did the extra hour come from? Did the planet stop its rotation for a full hour?? No, I think we would have noticed if it did. Especially if it was at night; you'd have been able to see the moon closing in on us at a rather frantic pace. I guess we should be thankful it wasn't the springtime change, where the earth would have had to rotate one hour instantaneously. With the laws of momentum and all, the only people that would have been safe would be the ones in an airplane at the time. If they were lucky!

Here's what I'm getting at. There's only one time, and if you're jumping from one hour to the next, at most, one of the times can be correct. In my example, that means it was either 3:44 PM or 2:44 PM. It could have been something altogether different, but for the sake of argument, let's say that one of them was in fact correct. If it was 3:44 PM, then there was no reason for the clocks to be changed. If it was 2:44 PM, then there was no point in waiting; The clocks should have just been changed to the correct time right then. I'm a salary worker, so my boss wouldn't have given a shit. He would have probably be thrilled getting an extra hour out of me for free.

To wrap this up, if there's some debate as to which is the correct time, just take the average of the two and call that the correct time. Make sure to broadcast it on TV and radio. Put it in the newspapers. Let everyone know that there's not going to be anymore seasonal clock-changing bullshit and if you're on daylight savings time, set your clock back a half hour, and if you're not, set it ahead a half hour. And quit fucking with the times!

FASHION PLATES

Here's something that's pissing me off: different schemes for license plates. Maybe it's the soon-to-be Geritol user in me speaking but I remember a day long ago that each state had one plate. Usually it was 2 colors: one for the background and one for the letters. Nice and simple. With a little bit of studying, you could easily get a glimpse at a license plate and know exactly which state it came from. But it isn't like that anymore. Noooo. Now each state has a fucking dozen different plate styles.

Save the Icelandic snow owls. Mothers against drunk driving, MADD or DAMM or whatever the hell it is. Bicentennial plates. DARE not to use drugs. If there's a cause that at least a half dozen people in the state might be remotely interested in, the state's gotta come out with a fucking license plate design for it! It has gotten so bad that unless you're right up on someone's ass, enough so that you can make out the name of the state printed on it, you have no fucking clue where the car is registered.

I'm just waiting to see a guy commit a hit and run. Some poor fuck crossing the street, listening to an iPod (playing the Awful Show naturally) and the guy driving in front of me nails him. The poor bastard flies 30 feet into the air and bounces off the ground like Silly Putty when he comes back down. The driver doesn't show any sign of stopping. So I call 911 and tell them what I saw. I tell them what kind of car it was, what color and everything. I give them the numbers on the license plate. And they ask me what state. "*I don't know. I don't have a fucking clue! Which state's license plate has Pee Wee Herman jacking off a bald eagle? Does that help narrow the selection any? Tell you what! Look for the car with those numbers on the plate and if the hood has the impression of a person's genitals in it, I'd say you found the guy*".

Here's yet another driving thing I've noticed. Did you ever get behind someone with a turn signal that's like a strobe light? I'm talking about a turn signal that blinks like 10 times a second. Jesus! Nothing like going into a seizure waiting for someone to make a turn!

A STORM BY ANY OTHER NAME WOULD BLOW AS HARD

When they name hurricanes, why do they give them American names? Every time a nautical twister rolls ashore, you hear on the news "Hurricane Charlie" or "Hurricane Hugo" or some other common name personifying the event. I would think for something with as much destructive power as a hurricane, they need to start giving these things middle eastern names, like terrorists. Which are you more likely to take serious: Hurricane Wilma or Hurricane Oussef-Ali?

Or if you feel that using terrorist-style names is a little too unpatriotic, you could always just give them less proper names. Hurricane Fist Fuck and Hurricane Scrotum Rip come to mind. If I hear that Hurricane Rita is rolling in, I'm inclined to not even go to the basement. If Hurricane Rectal Tear comes ashore, I'm getting the fuck out of Dodge!

THIS TOPIC IS JUST GAY

When gay kids go to a playground and use the swing set, do they straddle the swing and go left to right? Because I can tell you right now, I don't swing that way. Okay, that was pretty bad. But while I'm on the subject of homosexuality...

Go into a bar sometime, if you're a guy that is. This doesn't work as well if you're a woman. Go in and ask the bartender what the gayest "foo-foo" drink he knows how to make is.

He'll name something: Sex on the Beach, Cosmopolitan, Mojito, whatever. Say "okay make me one of those". Usually the temptation will be strong enough that the bartender will be unable to resist asking "are you gay". Then you can tell him. "No, I just have such an enormous penis that I'm secure enough about my masculinity to drink something like this". To be on the safe side, wear comfortable shoes in case you have to run when the guy pulls out a baseball bat from behind the bar.

RULES OF THE AIRWAVES

Entertainment is a lot different now than it was 20-30 years ago, but some rules still apply. I was a DJ when I was at Slippery Rock and I remember that we were given a very basic, very strict set of FCC guidelines before they'd let us on the air. The 2 big rules were that you couldn't say things that graphically described 1) excretive, or 2) sexual acts or body parts. Nowadays, it seems that even those rules have been thrown out the window. Well...they have and they haven't.

Like later at night on TV, after 10 PM or so, it isn't uncommon to hear the term 'asshole' during a show. The way most of us were brought up, we knew that was a pretty big curse word. But honestly it doesn't really break the rules. In a technical sense. Because it depends how the word is used. The rule says that you can't use it as you would in the sentence "That guy shoved a pool cue right up Tony's asshole". But it isn't often you hear the term 'asshole' to literally describe a person's anus. By extension, it's perfectly fine to say "That guy is an asshole for what he did to Tony!" because it's not used to relate to the anus. There aren't many people walking around whose bodies consist solely of anus.

Another word is the ever-popular 'shit'. George Carlin spoke out a while ago on this and he was correct when he said that 'shit' is used more figuratively than literally. Likewise on television, you don't hear a guy say "I'm going to take a shit", but it's passable if a guy says "what's this shit?". Unless of course he's referring to a pile of shit instead of saying it in reference to getting screwed over by a co-worker or what have you. So the whole deal is very complicated. But even back before you could say 'asshole' or 'shit' at all on TV, there were double standards that existed.

Take the word 'anus'. The rules said you couldn't say this on TV. Save for some of the medical documentaries on PBS and such. For the most part, stations would bleep out or over-dub such a usage. The reason being: it was considered an excretory body part. But when you think about it, a lot of similar words got past. Like 'colon'. The colon can certainly be considered an excretory organ, but the FCC didn't have a problem with someone saying their dad died from colon cancer. What about the small intestine, and for that matter, I think you could consider anything that's part of the GI tract part of the excretory system. After all, the anus is pretty useless without the stomach and intestines. And even if something is coming out of someone's anus, someone without a stomach and intestines, it's a fair bet that person doesn't have a pulse either. Technically speaking, you could go as far as saying the mouth is vital to digestion and excretion, couldn't you? And not only are you allowed to say 'mouth' on TV, you can show it, up close! I think it's only fair that if networks can show the mouth on TV that they also be allowed to show the anus. Though I hope that the powers that be have the decency to only show the anuses of healthy young women. Preferably ones who have recently undergone an anal bleaching procedure. There are just certain guidelines of taste that need to be observed.

THOSE WHO DANCE ARE CONSIDERED INSANE...

There's a song by Sly and the Family Stone called "Dance to the Music". Good song. Nice rhythm. But I have to question the verbiage. "Dance to the music"? As opposed to what? Dancing without the music? There are plenty of people who dance without the music, but usually they're living in the streets and are completely insane! I don't know of anyone of sound mind who dances when there is no music. What else would you dance to? Spoken word? I'm pretty sure if I ever knew someone who polkas while listening to Rush Limbaugh, I would have probably recommended they be committed a long time ago.

EXTENDED WARRANTY NOT AVAILABLE

With the economy slowly turning into a bedpan full of geriatric liquid shit, I have an idea that could be quite profitable. What you do is start a car company. Build all kinds, compacts, minivan, luxury, trucks, whatever. But here's the catch: offer cars with an unlimited lifetime warranty. No other car company in the history of the world has done that. Well, not successfully anyhow. With a selling point like that, cars will sell like crazy. Dealers won't be able to keep them in stock. Like the Wii. Then after about five years, you flat out close the company. You take the money and just walk away. There'll be no one to go to for warranty claims. If they try to come at you, you just tell them you don't work there anymore. You'll be a billionaire and retired after only 5 years of work. Fuck Social Security! You're independently wealthy!

DON'T PUT THAT IN YOUR MOUTH!

I was in the grocery store the other day and I saw they had Philly cream cheese in various flavors. Strawberry, pineapple, the cinnamon one sounded really good. But one of the flavors was salmon. What the fuck! Salmon flavored cream cheese?!? Ewwww!! Jesus! Why don't they just come out with vagina-flavored cream cheese?!? You could actually have a whole line of genital-flavored cream cheeses. Call them *Smegma Spreads*. Christ!

As I said once before in my Ambrosia salad sentiment, who the fuck eats this shit?!? I'm convinced that there's this whole race of people with absolutely no taste buds whatsoever. There has to be! Otherwise they wouldn't make this shit! There has got to be someone out there eating Spam! Fucking company has been making it for 70 goddamn years. Someone has to be buying it. Have you ever seen this shit? It looks like human penis meat for fuck's sake! I'm sure that there's some taboo cannibalistic appeal to it, but God almighty! There are people who regularly consume this.

Now, I know it isn't human penis meat. I checked it out. It's actually pork shoulder and ham meat. Pork shoulder. Imagine that. Here's a patent-named food product based on pig shoulder. And not just a food! There's a whole industry. A fucking industry based on this culinary abomination. The varieties! They make hot and spicy Spam. With Tabasco. Which I think could be one of the more intelligent moves actually. Try to take a person's mind off of what they're actually consuming by lighting their tongue on fire. They make Spam with bacon. For those who don't feel that regular Spam clogs their arteries enough by itself, I suppose. Spam with cheese. Oh, here's a good idea! Take something that looks like penis meat and throw little chunks of cheese in it! Did you ever take cheesecake and smear it over a woman's pussy and then eat her out? No? There's a good fucking reason for that! But the Spam people apparently don't care. They make garlic Spam. I guess if you want to chow down on unappetizing canned meat AND keep vampires away, they're looking out for you. And then there's turkey Spam. Turkey. Okay, let me try to figure this one out. Spam is made from pork shoulder, right? Okay, so what the fuck is turkey Spam made from?? You ever seen a turkey? They don't even have fucking shoulders!! Which really messed me up, because if regular Spam looks like penis meat, does turkey Spam look like a Turkish guy's penis?? Awww, fucking shit! I just tasted vomit. What the fuck is wrong with people that they can't just eat a fucking hamburger and be happy. God dammit!

OH, FOR CHRIST'S SAKE!

Jimmy Hoffa, Jim Morrison, Elvis Presley and Jesus Christ: What do all 4 of these guys have in common? Let's have a look.

All of them begin with a "J". Oh, wait. No. Elvis doesn't. Scratch that.

All of them are guys. Well, yeah. but so is 49% of the planet, so that's not really anything.

Hmmm. Thinking, thinking, thinking...

Well, Jimmy Hoffa is dead. He bribed a grand juror. Next thing you know he's part of the foundation in one of the endzones of Giants Stadium. Poor fuck. But that's what you get when you play with the Mafia.

Jim Morrison? Dead. He paid a visit to Mr. Bubble in France and never came home.

Elvis Presley? Poor Elvis. Died in the worst place possible. On the shitter! I just hope someone flushed for him. That's one type of keepsake that's better let go of!

And Jesus. Yes, he too is dead. Died a looooong time ago. Close to 2,000 years ago as a matter of fact. And despite certain popular opinions, he **did not** come back. Died from a combination of asphyxiation, dehydration and blood loss. Nasty way to go for sure. But he did not rise from the dead. I know this is a shock to all the Christians out there who have spent their lives believing it, but it's true.

When he was alive, he was a remarkable man! There's no denying that! He was an amazing teacher. A lot of his life lessons are very useful to this day. He was a healer, though not necessarily as miraculous as folks have been lead to believe. A lot of his healing was more psychological than anything. Lots of hypochondriacs back in the old days. Faith healers could have cleaned up back then!

But the fact remains, he was just a man. He was not the son of God. Sorry.

"RAPE ME, MY FRIEND" ADDENDUM

Now that I've given women the chance to develop a deep, burning hatred for me...

It seems that a lot of people have gotten the impression that I was saying 'if a woman gets fucked up on a date and she gets raped, it's her own fault'. I haven't the slightest fucking clue how anyone could come to this conclusion based on what I said. That would seem to be a form of 'semantic rape', because my original message got fucked!

Here's the deal. If a woman says 'no', it's rape. It's not 'date rape' or 'acquaintance rape' or anything like that. It's plain fucking rape! If a woman says 'yes' initially, then changes her mind and says 'no' when it's about to happen (or even while it's happening) and the man doesn't stop, that too is rape. Now, here's the part I want to be absolutely clear on. If a woman says 'yes' and doesn't give any indication of resistance or saying 'no' before or during, but **afterward** says that she was raped because she didn't actually want it to happen, *then* it should not be called rape. If this lack of resistance or contradiction is due to booze or drugs, **it shouldn't make a difference**!! Men can't read minds. I don't give a fuck what certain 'psychics' claim to be able to do, it isn't possible! Unless the woman gives some sort of outward indication that she does not want it to happen, and that can be verbal like saying 'no' or even something as simple as pushing the man away or turning away or whatever, the man has no way of knowing that it's something she doesn't want. For the record, laying there motionless and/or watching TV during does not count. Ever been married?

And as a personal note, I would never rape a woman. I don't care how slutty she dressed or how seductive she was or even if she was wearing spandex, I would never put my dick in a woman if I wasn't perfectly clear that it's what she wanted. If she changed her mind during (I don't care if it was on the first thrust or 2 seconds before climax), I would stop immediately. I don't care if my balls turn into fucking blueberries, I would cease and desist that second! Any man who wouldn't do the same is simply not a man, and should have their cocks removed by an International Harvester and suffer a life of daily sodomy until the day they die.

I hope that helps clarify things.

I HATE TO BE ANAL ABOUT THIS...

I know I'm fighting a losing battle with this one, but I have to at least try to sway popular usage a bit. When someone follows a personal methodology strictly and in an unwavering fashion, they should be said to be **retentive**, not *anal*. The full term is "anal retentive", a phrase coined by Sigmund Freud. It comes from his theory of psychosexual development wherein at a certain age a child is said to gain a sexual pleasure from holding in feces. Yeah. Freud was a pretty sick fuck. No argument there. But regardless, the correct abridged version of that term is simply retentive. Not anal. Anal is a sexual act. When you call someone anal, you're actually saying that they like it up the ass. While that may or may not be true, it has absolutely nothing to do with keeping a clean work area or writing a document or any of a million other things you fuckers are trying the imply that a person does with a lack of flexibility. In fact when you call someone anal, you're actually implying they have flexibility. Well, in at least one area.

YOU AIN'T THE BOSS OF ME!

Another fucked up lyric. Bruce Springstein's "Dancing in the Dark": *You can't start a fire without a spark.* Ever heard of combustion??

And why is he called "The Boss". The boss of what? Himself?? So he's self-employed. Big fucking whoop. A lot of people are self-employed. Doesn't make him special.

And what the fuck, pray tell, is a PANK Cadillac?? Not pink, PANK! For fuck's sake, you're from New Jersey, not Alabama! Speak English!

KEYZ'S X-RATED ALPHABET

I've decided that I would make an awesome producer for a late-night educational program on PBS. While I try to convince the network execs of this, enjoy my take on the teaching of the alphabet.

A: Angry African-American antagonists are assholes.
B: Big Bulgarian bitches blow beastly belches.
C: Consuming circumcised cocks can cause cancer.
D: Dirty donkey dildos don't do dick.
E: Every elephant erection expels enormous ejaculations.
F: Fat, flaming faggots feel fashionable frequently.
G: Gangrenous gonads generally grow green.
H: Handsome historians handle hairy hooters hourly.
I: Ignorance initially increases intestinal irritability.
J: Jewish judges jerk-off Japanese jurors.
K: Korean kids kick kosher kittens' kidneys.
L: Lonesome losers loves licking librarian labia.
M: My maid masturbates many midnights.
N: Nasty nuts naturally nauseate neurotic Negroes.
O: Old oriental officers occasionally orgasm openly.
P: Pasty pussy probably pees pretty putrid piss.
Q: Queer queens quiff quite quietly.
R: Rowdy, religious rednecks really reek, right?
S: Surprisingly, sloppy seconds seriously sickens some.
T: Those tarantula testicles tasted terrible today.
U: Unkempt, unionized undertakers usually utilize urine.
V: Very vulgar villains violently violate virgin vagina.
W: Willy Wonka wishes wanking wasn't wasteful.
X: eXtreme eXistentialists eXamine eXcrement eXtensively. (Gimme a break. It's fucking 'X'!)
Y: Your Yorkie yacked Yoohoo yawning yesterday.
Z: Zipperhead zoologists zombified zebra zygotes zealously.

PLUG UP THE DYKE

I guess there's some kind of scale regarding homosexuality. I'm curious though.

Is the woman who wears the strap-on more of a lesbian than the one who receives? Unless they take turns regularly, I figure that would have to hold true. After all, the woman receiving is having the same experience (or at least very similar) that she would have with a guy. That to me would indicate low-level lesbianism (or LLL). On the other hand, the woman who is playing the role of the man (AKA the "bull dyke", the "diesel dyke", or what have you) would seem to have a higher concentration of carpet muncher in her.

Just a thought.

SAVE MY UNCHANGED BALLS!

This has been pissing me off for a long time. In Micro$oft Word, when you open up some documents only to print them, then go to close them, it asks you if you want to save changes before closing.

What the fuck?!? **What** fucking changes?!? Am I the only person this happens to?? I opened the fucking document, I printed it, I closed it. I didn't change a goddamn thing? What the fuck do you think you're saving?!? Does my computer now keep track of shit that I printed, so that when I open it later, that annoying fucking worthless paperclip pops up and tells me "Hey, you already printed this document. Would you like help printing it again?" Fuck you, paperclip! If I want to print the cocksucker 50 times, I will. Since when does a digital paperclip have an Earth-friendly social conscience??

I'm going to take that fucking paperclip, straighten it out, and shove it up Rosie O'Donnell's fat fucking cellulite-infested, shit-caked ass! Whose idea was it at Micro$oft to make a little animated paperclip to ask you stupid fucking questions when the regular help system was perfectly easy to use?!? Do people need to have this shit personified at every fucking turn? Fuck the paperclip, fuck Bill Gates, and fuck Micro$oft "Would-you-like-to-save-the-changes-even-though-you-didn't-actually-make-any-fucking-changes?" Word!

DEW ME, BABY!

I'm a Mountain Dew junkie. Most times I get the Cubes (24 pack). Occasionally I get the 12-packs. They used to have 3x4 12-packs, but now they're all 2x6. When they first went to that standard, the packs said "Fits in your fridge"! I thought about this and realized that wasn't saying much. I can fit the 24-pack in the fridge on the top shelf. Hell, if you take the racks out, you could fit a fairly large person in the fucking thing! Not much of a selling point if you ask me. Maybe that's why they don't put it on there anymore.

MOTHER'S MILK

Don't worry. The title does not imply any content about lactation. It was simply Mother's Day when I came up with this and I'm talking about milk, so...

I don't know where the fuck bag boys are getting the idea that I don't want my gallon of milk in a bag just like the rest of my groceries! And if there's a concern about the weight of the thing breaking through the bag, then fucking double bag it! Sweet fucking Christ! How do these people not understand that, if it fits in a bag, it should be put in a bag! The canned tomatoes go in a bag. The 90 lb. bag of dog food doesn't. The creamed eel scrotum goes in a bag. The bundle of 16-foot 2x4s doesn't. The 28 lb. box of kitty litter doesn't go in a bag. **The fucking gallon of milk does!!**

Then I hear some people say "It has it's own handle". This is really fucking stupid. A coffee mug has a handle. When was the last time you bought a coffee mug and they didn't give you a bag for it?? Hell! In some of the nicer places, they'll actually put the cup in a box first, and then put the box in a bag!

Another thing: There is milk in the handle. Every brand of milk I've ever gotten a gallon of (except the old fashioned kind with the red "overhead" handle) has a hollow handle on the side with milk in it. Which means if you're holding the thing for more than 60 seconds, it not only makes your hand cold. It makes the milk in the handle warm! Have you ever tasted warm milk. Great to help you sleep, but it tastes fucking awful! And it doesn't keep well, unless you enjoy making your own cottage cheese.

So you fuckers with the name tag and acne earning $4 an hour: Put my fucking milk in a fucking bag!

ATHEIST BIRDS

I'm not sure if this is proof positive that God doesn't exist or if it's simply an indication that all birds go to hell. Take the "Christ the Redeemer" statue on Corcovado Mountain in Rio. You know the one. Big ass statue of Jesus with his arms spread. Do you realize how much bird shit is all over that statue? This either means that God doesn't exist (if he did, wouldn't it be in his interest to bestow some magical force that keeps shit off the statue?) or that birds go to hell for desecrating it.

Now a third possibility. Maybe there is a God, but defecation is not an affront to sacred elements. If that's true, where's the line drawn? Is it okay to take a shit in the collection plate when they pass it in church?

Do I give the impression that I need to find a hobby?

MERRY SEXMAS!

Winter Wonderland Lyrics: "In the meadow we can build a snowman, then pretend that he is Parson Brown. He'll say: Are you married? We'll say: No man, but you can do the job when you're in town".

"You can do the job when you're in town". Am I the only one who that sounds blatantly sexual to? I know it's an Xmas classic and all, but still I can only picture the person (who is saying that to the snowman) bending over and pointing to a welcoming orifice as they do.

I'm a disturbed man.

SPIT IT OUT!

What is it with all these fucking pop songs with the stuttering?!? "*Puh-Puh-Puh-Poker Face*". "*Blame it on the A-a-a-a-a-alcohol*".

You know what I say? *Tuh-tuh-tuh-tuh-tuh-today, Junior!*

Music has gotten so fucking lazy! Like these assholes who think that it's creative to rhyme any word that ends in a long 'O' sound with "Yo"! I wonder what sound they'd make if I went ahead and kicked them in the nuts. They'd probably just make up a word to rhyme. That's how the whole -izzle shit got started.

ISN'T THAT TWEET?

I've been busy on The Awful Show's own answer to Twitter. Here's a recap of my postings there.

- 2nd to last ingredient in Mountain Dew: Brominated vegetable oil. What the fuck?!?
- Life is to 'complicated' as love is to 'clusterfuck'.
- Monday: from Old English monedæi, meaning the day the mind turns to tapioca.
- Ho-Down: The cunnilingus equivalent of a Brojob.
- Keyz's Irresponsible Tip #143: Nothing gets rid of that squiggly line in your sight faster than a nail gun.

- To Bruegger's Bagels, Re: Plastic knives to cut bagels . . . Oh, you guys are hilarious!! What a riot!! Fuckers.
- If the word 'baby' did not exist, Britney couldn't sing. She would just stand on stage for 2 hours.
- Speaking of Britney, do the lyrics of 'If U Seek Amy' make anyone else want to just punch her in the cunt?
- Feminist Thought Of The Day: Men suck!
- When a retarded person goes insane, do they do it slower? Wouldn't that be a good thing?
- What do you call it when you're fondled by the doctor during your vasectomy? . . . Snipping and handling. (Failed joke from Show 164)
- I need to catch up with my net lingo. For a while I thought 'FTW' was just 'WTF' backward. 'Fuck the What'?!? Strange.
- It's sad when the peak of happiness in my life is getting 2 Snickers instead of 1 because of a miscalibration in the snack machine.
- ringringringringringringring...banana phone! Damn that infectious song!!
- When you get to level 50 on Facebook's 'Farmville', I think you should be able to grow pot.
- Suicide is literally a means to an end.
- What do you get when you mix urine with ranch dressing? You get piss-flavored dressing! What the hell did you think you would get?!?
- 'They' should change the name of the dice game from 'Farkle' to 'Fuckhole', cause that's what I always end up yelling!
- Why do we use the term 'douche bag' to insult each other? Why not 'maxi-pad'? How about 'feminine hygiene spray'?

- Black Power is inspirational. White Power is racist. Can someone explain that shit to me?!?
- If, in the term 'strange bird', the size of the bird is proportional to the strangeness, I must work with an ostrich!
- The term 'Southern Cross'. Doesn't it sound like two perpendicular pieces of wood, aflame on a black guy's lawn?

GETTING RAILED

I was stopped at a railroad crossing the other day. As the train went by, I noticed one of the cars has a sign on it that read "Do Not Hump". Is a sign like this even necessary?!? While I may be one of the hornier and more sexually-liberal people on the planet, even I have my limits. Jesus!

NO FREE PARKING

Parking for pregnant women is bullshit. Why should women get special treatment for not being able to keep their legs closed? What about special parking for big, fat fucks? You know, people who can't keep their hands off the crullers and Ben and Jerry's. I think if they have parking for pregos, they should have the same for lardos. The principle is pretty much the same. It's just in the case of fat people, it's a different orifice and it is stuff is going *into* the body that can't be helped. Actually, bulging pregnant broads *had* something going in, but that was several months prior.

Maternity leave is another thing. What the fuck is that all about? I mean...okay, maybe it can be considered time off for an injury. If I ever shit a bowling ball, I would probably insist on some time off too. But it should count as vacation time. Or an unpaid leave. Unless the chick got knocked up by her boss, the company should not pay her for her time off. And she gets a week off. That's it. After a week, if she doesn't come back to work, fire the whore. Then she can take all the time she wants to be a sperm dumpster.

CINE-MUNCHABLES

Why do they serve popcorn and candy at the movie theater? Why don't they have other foods? I think macaroni and cheese would be good while watching a movie. Or if that has too much potential to be messy, how about popcorn chicken and shrimp? Of course at the movie theater, they'd have to offer a 2 pound bucket that costs $197. Just for consistency, you know.

KISS MY ROOTS!

I can't imagine I'll be winning any popularity contests with this one, but I need to get it out.

Affirmative action is bullshit!

I did a little research. Turns out that slavery was abolished in 1865. That means that if there was a person who was a slave for one day when they were born, the day before the abolition, to be alive today they'd be the tender age of 144! The record for the oldest living human was 122 years old. So it's safe to say that anyone that affirmative action is meant to "make it up to" isn't alive to appreciate it. And as for making it up to their descendants, that's a fucking crock! My ancestors could have done some truly atrocious things. That in no way makes me accountable. I don't give a shit if my great-grandfather was Hitler! I wasn't even alive when the Holocaust went down. Therefore I don't owe shit to anyone!

Black people are even better off than white people nowadays. Oh, pick your jaw up off the floor; I'm going to explain. Here's the thing: no matter how bad job markets get and no matter how high the cost of everything soars, black people can become rap stars. White people can't pull that off (save for a few minor exceptions that had incredible timing. *cough* Vanilla Ice *cough*). And with something like rap, you don't even have to have any talent!

You certainly don't need to be able to sing. That much is obvious. There are plenty of black people that sing; don't misunderstand. Beyonce has an incredible voice. But that isn't rap. You could be the most tone deaf motherfucker in the world (and notice that the word "deaf" has an 'a' in it. Thank you), and you can still rap.

Some might argue that you need to have rhythm. That's another load of shit. Have you ever really listened to Snoop Dogg? Unless he's intentionally getting off rhythm (and why the fuck would he do that?!?), that isn't what I would call 'tight'. *A'ight?*

Speaking of rhyming (heh-heh), you don't even need to be able to fucking rhyme to do rap. If you need to put together two lines that don't end with similar sounding words, all you need to do is take the first letter of each last word and add

'-iggity' to it. Or '-izzle', or some other collection of letters that make the words more nonsensical than half of the Dr. Seuss titles available.

In this country, all people should have equality. That's fine. I don't have a problem with equality. **But!**...to all the black people out there who think they're owed something just for being black, go fuck yourselves.

LEAD(ERSHIP) POISONING

I'm a nerd. A geek. A spaz. A poindexter. A...well, you get the idea. I always have been, too. I don't know if everyone has experienced this at one time or another in school, but I know whenever teachers would leave the room for a moment, they'd leave a student *in charge*. One who was a teacher's pet, so to speak. Naturally, as you have probably already deduced, that was me.

I haven't been in school for a long time, but just recently I've come up with a speech that would have been very useful for these occasions. Whenever the teacher would ask me to watch the class, I would reply with...

"Thanks, but no thanks. You see, by choosing me, it's implied that I'm one who is trustworthy as I take my studies seriously. But as you may know, the amount of seriousness with one's schooling is inversely proportional to one's popularity. Anything I do to keep order with the class once you walk out the door will be deftly ignored. The result will be chaos. And if I'm so inclined to report those who ignore my effort, the result will surely be me getting pummeled to a mass of bleeding flesh and fractured bone after 3:15 PM. So, while I appreciate your confidence in me, I have to decline the offer. You'll just have to wait until lunch to change your tampon".

That last part would probably have gotten me detention, but it would most surely have bumped my popularity up at least a point or two.

WHEELIN' AND DEALIN'

On my way home from visiting my mom one day, I had the little plastic wheel for Mario Kart in the car. On a whim, I decided to actually steer the car with the bottom of the real steering wheel, but with the other hand, I held up and made it appear that I was steering with the Mario Kart wheel. I figure even if I only freaked one person out that day, it was worth the effort.

OUR FEATURING PRESENTATION

What is it with these rap artists who always have to feature someone else? T-Pain featuring Ludacris. R. Kelly featuring Li'l Jon. Extra Crispy featuring Chocolate Cream Parfait! Are we to assume by this that these assholes don't have enough talent to do this shit by themselves? That they have to subcontract additional talent just to be able to make a decent single? Here's something you may want to look into: **forming a band**! Bel Biv Devoe was 3 different guys. Individually, they only had a third of the talent needed to make a hit. What did they do? Formed a group! One of them didn't feel the egotistical need to be headlined over the others. They didn't feel the need to have one guy with the others just being "featured". If you can't do it by yourself, quit fucking putting your name above everyone else's, you egomaniacal douchebags!

WEATHER OR NOT

Here's a question: Does Seattle even have a meteorologist? And if they do, what's the point?? I've never been out there but I can imagine what the news would sound like.

News Guy: ...And now here's Hal Storm with today's weather.
Hal: Rain.
News Guy: Uh-huh. And how about tomorrow.
Hal: Rain.
News Guy: Oh. Dare I ask about the 5-day forecast?
Hal: (takes another drink) Rain, rain, rain, rain, and more f-(bleep)-king rain!
News Guy: Well, thanks Hal. Next up: Sports.

EXTRA CHEESE IN WAYNESBURG

Only in fucking Waynesburg! On my way home one day, there was a guy standing in the middle of the road, a main road mind you (2 lanes, 1 way), holding a pizza sign! "Large cheese pizza! Five Bucks!"...in the middle of the fucking street! You know something? I hoped someone would hit him! I hope the son of a bitch gets run right the fuck over! Then they'll have to change the sign to read "Road Pizza"!

A REDNECKS-PERIMENT

Because they're such an easy target, I don't like to bash on Southern people...no, that's not true. I love bashing them! But think about the people in the south. Do you ever get the feeling that they're actually an experiment conducted by the government? Like 400 years ago, they cryogenically froze some of these genetic defectives with top-secret technology, and then they just thawed them about 30 or 40 years ago to see how they'd react to a more modern existence? That's my guess.

ANOREX-IDIOCY

Here's a stupid concept: Size 0. What the fuck is a size zero?!? Whose moronic idea was it to create a dress size less than 1?? Wouldn't it make sense to have Size 1 be the base line? Zero implies non-existence. How many gods are there? Zero. See? And where the fuck do you get a dress makers' dummy in a Size 0 anyway? What, do they just use a coat rack? They need to correct these sizes. I don't think it should be all that hard. Say Karen Carpenter is a size 1, then roll from there.

GENERATION GRIPE

I'd like to know who came up with the empty sentiment "Respect your elders". When was the last time someone older than yourself, other than a family member, showed you respect? When was the last time an elderly person gave up their seat on the bus so a younger person could sit down?

Keep that in mind next time you're driving and one of these Geritol-gobbling, Depends customers is going through the crosswalk in front of you at a blistering pace of 5 miles a decade when the light says "Don't Walk". Fuck old people! Fuck them in their wrinkled old asses!

CRUNCH TIME!

Here's something I think that would be awesome to see: Two tractor trailers, fully loaded, in a head-on collision at 80 miles per hour...**But!** Between them you put a Ford Festiva. Wouldn't that be a blast? And then, on that same thought, you could have competitions. It would be the hottest new redneck sport! Teams of 2 guys could compete to see how vertically thin they could make the Festiva. I'd even buy a ticket to that shit. This would also work with a Toyota Camry, by the way.

IS THAT SOME KIND OF JOAQ?...OR...JOAQ THIS WAY

Sorry. I couldn't decide on a title. Now, then...

I've had it with certain names people have, like this Joaquin Phoenix. What the fuck kind of name is that? And how the fuck is it pronounced "Wah-keen"? Who came up with that stupid shit?!? Pronounce it the way it's fucking spelled, you arrogant prick! "Joe-Ah-Kwin". That's how it should sound! The fucking pompousness of these Hollywood cocks! Though it would be fun to be a cobbler and be making a pair of boots for him. Then you could actually say "These boots are made for 'Wah-keen'". Yeah. Pretty bad way to end that. Fuck it.

INSTANT LOSER

At the time of this writing, it has been about six months since the last McDonald's Monopoly game was in play. And wouldn't you know, I'm **still** finding those fucking game pieces in my car!

I'm going to say this one last time. I **will not** play the McDonald's Monopoly game any more! Not this year and not ever again! You know what happens? I end up with 800 loose pieces in every crack and crevice at home, at work and in the car, and every fucking one of them is either Oriental Avenue or Park Place! And one would think "*Oh my god! Park Place! All I need is Boardwalk now and I win $1,000,000*"! Give me a small fucking personal break! Do people not realize that in order to have any chance at getting Boardwalk, you would need to eat at McDonald's 5 or 6 times a day? And even if you do win, all that money is going straight for your open heart surgery anyway! And if by some chance there's anything left after they remove fucking Mayor McCheese from your aorta, the rest of it would be needed for home renovations to widen the doorways of your house so you can get your fat ass in and out of the fucking place. Bullshit!

From now on, any time I get McDonald's and there's a game piece on it, it's getting thrown away, unpeeled, with the empty cup or box. I don't care if it's an instant winner for a free small fries or a million dollars. If some bum digging through the land fill finds it, good for him! Let him win whatever I throw away. Anyone willing to dig through filth and garbage looking for stuff just to survive has earned it as far as I'm concerned.

Fuck McDonald's, and fuck Monopoly for that matter!

NEW KEYZ-TIONARY ENTRY

paleneck (n.) - someone who lives in a redneck area and is surrounded by rednecks, but refuses to succumb to becoming a redneck themselves.

MUSIC TO MY EARS

Here's a great marketing idea for the music industry. Have Kevin Federline and Justin Timberlake make an album together and call it "Douches Wild". I think it would sell great considering some of the shit you can hear on any number of radio stations. Of course, nowadays you would be able to hear it crystal clear with the whole HD radio thing coming into play. You know what would really be a huge step for technology? Creating a device you could attach to your radio that would make the music it plays good! Come to think of it, they do have such a device. It's called an iPod.

THE NAME OF THE GAME

No matter how much you hate your name, it could always be worse. There's a boxer from Thailand with the name Terdsak Jandaeng. Yes, you read that right. His first name is pronounced "Turd Sack". What the fuck kind of a nickname would you develop with something like that? 'Colostomy Bag'??

But on the other side of that, one has to remember that this may be a very noble name in Thailand. English names aren't all that big there. There are plenty of names in the English-speaking countries that could be dirty with a small change. And I'm not talking about Dick and Peter. Those are just filthy to begin with. But a name like...Enis. There are actually people who have the name 'Enis'. This has got to be one of the hardest names to grow up with. It's a double whammy. First of all it sounds way too much like "anus". And then, if you add a 'p' at the beginning, you've got 'Penis'! One name, four little letters, and you've got 'penis' and 'anus'!! Of course, it's appropriate it comes out like that, cause quite obviously with a name like 'Enis', from day one, you're fucked in the ass!

ALCOHO-LICK MY ASS!

I've developed a true spite for made-up words that end in '-holic'. Unless there's a form of whatever the first part of the word is that chemically has oxygen-hydrogen (-OH) branches, it's a bullshit word. Words like 'workaholic', 'sexaholic', and 'shopaholic' are completely and totally bogus. This is pretty obvious when you break down the work 'alcoholic'. First things last. The '-ic' comes from the Latin '-icus', meaning 'of or pertaining to'. When alcohol (the first part) becomes such a consuming factor that it becomes part of their very being, said person is considered to be an alcoholic. So the proper form of the 3 aforementioned literary atrocities would be 'workic', 'sexic' and 'shopic'. They may not sound as pretty, but at least they're correct! And if you're going to start in with that "it's a contemporary suffix" horseshit, you can take out a piece of stationary, write the word 'dick' on it, and fucking eat it! Contemporary is a euphemism for 'made up by modern jackoffs'.

A FIRST AMENDMENT ADDENDUM

An up-until-now unwritten rule: Any musical artist who has less fans than people who passionately hate them is forbidden from performing. With the internet, this shouldn't be very difficult to figure out with a central, well-secured voting system. Make a website, promote it and let people vote whether they love or hate all the various artists. If an artist is below 50% in the "loved" category, they're not allowed to perform until that improves. They can do whatever it takes. Volunteer work, donating to various causes, or what have you. Now, naturally, Lindsay Lohan is exempt from this rule. I think she's hot. Since this is my law, I get to declare the exceptions as I see fit.

CARTOONS REALLY DO LEAD TO VIOLENCE

I must have really had some serious anger issues as a young kid. There's this animation production company called The DIC company (pronounced "Deek"). The initials stood for "Diffusion, Information et Communication". I'm guessing by the 'et' that it was a French company. That alone was probably my reason for hating them, but how strange it was that I felt this spite at such a young age. Anyway, the company produced some fairly well-known shows. Captain Planet, G. I. Joe, and Inspector Gadget just to name a few of the bigger ones. And I enjoyed the shows too. But it never failed that when the show was over, the credits would roll, and right after the big "DIC" would appear and you would hear this little kid's voice say "Deek". And without fail I would go into a fucking tirade! *"It's Dick, you little faggot! Like what I'm going to rip off of you and beat you to death with!! SAY IT RIGHT, YOU LITTLE SHIT BASTARD"*!! I get the feeling I should have been locked into a mental health clinic much sooner than I actually was. Don't you?

@ THE LIMITS OF MY ¢ENSES

You know what has gained immense popularity since the internet came into widespread use? The @ sign. Did you ever use this thing before you started writing e-mails??

It's just a show of my age, but I remember way back to a time where typewriters used to have a cent (¢) key. Does anyone else remember this? Now if you want to use the cent sign on your word processor (because who the hell uses typewriters any more), you need to either go into the character map program or punch in some complex key sequence. It isn't hard to see why it's no longer a separate key though. Back when it was a key, you could actually do something with less than a buck.

THE SMELL OF SUCCESS

Don't you think it would be in the interest of various fast food establishments that have a distinctive smell (Long John Silver's comes to mind) to manufacture air fresheners? I think that this would be brilliant! They wouldn't even have to sell them. Just give them away in every bag. I'm convinced that they'd drive people into a frenzy. You would have people eating there 7 or 8 times a day. In a year, you would have people gaining 150 pounds. Type 2 diabetes would reach epidemic rates. Heart attacks at age 30 would be commonplace. But hey, fuck it. That's the business world.

TRAIL-ER BLAZING

Here's something fun to do. Next time you're driving and you see someone who has a horse trailer (with a horse in it preferably - this isn't as funny when the trailer is empty), pull in front of them and then slam on the brakes. The horse will go flying into the front of the trailer and just start going fucking bananas! It's even more fun to do with a whole trailer full of cows. Did I mention I love animals? Heh-heh-heh.

A MOIST ADJECTIVE

You know a really stupid word? Muggy. Who made up this word? What was wrong with the word 'humid'? I think it was just fine. It described that atmospheric condition well. And then some asshole meteorologist has to come up with 'muggy'. It doesn't even sound like it should have anything to do with humidity. It sounds like it should be in reference to a mug-shot-like appearance. Say you go to get your picture taken for your driver's license. The night before, you drank a case and a half of beer because your girlfriend left you. Right after cleaning out your bank account, that is. You passed out on your jacket and now you have the impression of a zipper all the way up your face on the right side. Your eyes look like you went swimming in a pool that was filled with brine instead of water. In short, you're a fucking mess! You go to get your picture taken. When you get it back, it looks like a picture that would be taken after the cops arrested you for drunk driving. It looks like a *mug shot*. Wouldn't it make sense to refer to the appearance of that photograph as being 'muggy'? It sure as hell seems a lot more appropriate a use than in describing a damp August day.

HOW TO GET A COUNTRY TO HATE YOU IN SIX LINES

I've written a good number of parodies for the podcast in a little over 3 years. Over the course of those parodies, I've probably offended about 90% of the English-speaking population. And yes I'm proud of that number, but I digress. A little while back I had just finished one parody and had an idea for another as I was coming home from work that night. I decided to see if the "iron was still hot". I heard Bad Company's "Rock and Roll Fantasy" which starts like this...

Here come the jesters, 1 2 3.
It's all part of my fantasy.
I've love the music
And I love to see the crowd.
Dancing in the aisles,
And singin' out loud.....Yeah

And I thought it would be cool to do "Anime Fantasy" that talks about how classic cartoons have taken a backseat to Japanese-styled anime. Here's what I started with...

Here come the Jetsons, George and Jane.
Since he got neutered, Astro ain't the same.
What could have happened

to derail this cartoon.
It's just like 9-11...
Oh, shit! Too soon??...Yeah!!

After that, I just quit. There's no way there wouldn't be backlash for that!! So that's one parody that has been averted. Sunrise, sunset.

A NEW LEVEL OF MALPRACTICE

They say that laughter is the best medicine. I got a migraine one afternoon. I forced myself to laugh for a half hour and nothing changed. So I took Advil. Within 15 minutes it went away. So much for that fucking theory.

But I was thinking about this. I think it would be a lot of fun to be the administrator of a hospital for just one day. And just one reason really. I would like to see a hospital try crazy straw catheters. Could you imagine the look on a patient's face when you tell them you're going to insert a catheter and pull out this tube that has six different turns in it?? It may increase the incidence of stress-induced heart attacks, but it would definitely be worth a laugh!

THE POT AND THE KETTLE

In this day and age, it's too much to expect the government to legalize marijuana, but can't they at least meet halfway? Like making possession a misdemeanor instead of a felony? Just a thought.

I really shouldn't have mentioned that because now I'm going to go off on a rant. Sigh.

Here's the deal: I do not use marijuana, but I still feel it should be legalized. I've tried marijuana twice. The first time I did, it was just after a break-up. My heart was broken, so I figured I would try to break my central nervous system to match. You know how that goes. I drank 8 beers in about 25 minutes. So I had a bit of a buzz. Then my friend mentions that they're going to go down the hall (I was in a dorm at the time. Guess that would help to mention) to smoke some weed. I go with them because at that point I would have run my nuts through a pasta maker if someone told me it would make me feel better. So I have a few hits. Didn't really have an effect on top of the massive amount of alcohol flowing though my system already. About 10 minutes later, I start to feel sick. I almost made it to the bathroom before my GI tract threw everything into full reverse. When I finally get there, I kneel down, lay my arm across the toilet seat, put my forehead on my arm and I stayed there for the better of 4 hours. I probably fell asleep a few times in that period.

The second time I tried it, I was drunk again. Only this time, it didn't make me sick. But yet again, it didn't help enhance the alcohol any. After that, I just never bothered with it. But I'm still of the mind that it should be legalized. My thought on why it isn't: Because it's too hard for the government to regulate.

Think of tobacco. That other stuff people smoke. How many people grow their own tobacco. Not a whole lot! It's because tobacco has a relatively small frame of conditions in which it can thrive. It needs to be warm and moist. The Carolinas? Excellent place to grow tobacco. Anchorage, Alaska? Not so good. So the government doesn't need to scour the whole country making sure every tobacco leaf grown goes through them. Marijuana on the other hand, you can grow damn near anywhere. That's why they call it *weed*! You can't stop it from growing any easier than dandelions! So instead of a small region to monitor, the government would have to monitor a much larger area to keep the taxes rolling in. What do they do? They say *'fuck it'* and just make it illegal. They wait until their herd of law enforcement sheep stumble upon it and then punish whoever's Cheetos-stained fingers are on the bag. Then they get to have the bail money **and** keep the pot!

America...the best country money can buy.

ALWAYS ROOTING FOR SECOND PLACE

This is just a little peculiarity about me. If you're ever at the track, and you hear that I bet on a horse, you should **never** bet on that same horse. My decision-making has proven to be inferior on a history-making level.

When I was a teenager and I wanted a VCR, I bought a Beta because I heard they had superior quality over VHS and, at the time, there were lots of video rental places that rented Beta cassettes. About a month later, you would think that the format never existed. When it was Christmas in 1989 (if memory serves) and I wanted a video game system, I asked for the Sega Master System. I was a big fan of the arcade game "R-Type" and that was the only system it was on. A month later they stopped making games for it en masse in favor of the good old 8-bit NES (The system that put Nintendo on the map). Even when I was much younger, I asked for GoBots instead of Transformers. People would think I have some kind of gypsy curse. Or maybe just the inability on a genetic level to pick "*the winner*".

I'm a video gamer for life. I've owned the 3DO, the Dreamcast and the Sega Saturn. And I probably would have had a 32X if money wasn't a problem at the time. When the next generation of game systems comes out, I'll make it known which one I plan on getting so everyone can make the smart decision and buy 'the other one'. Consider it a public service.

DRIVE SOMEONE CRAZY? CHECK!

Here's something fun to do. Whenever you write a check, after you write however many cents are included, add another zero (in other words, add zero tenths of a cent). People will look at that thing for a good minute before they can figure out what the fuck you wrote. And for added fun, when you write out the XX/100 of a dollar in the part you put the value spelled out, put the fractions of a dollar in terms of something other than 100. If it's an even number, put the fraction in terms of 50. It will make the accounting guy lose his fucking mind! You can actually give a person a permanent facial tic if you put the fraction in terms of pi. In this case, carrying a conversion chart is recommended for the sake of accuracy. Or how about this? Put the value of the check in equation form. The next time you write a check for $20, break it up into seventeen parts. "4 dollars plus 6 dollars minus 2 dollars plus 460 cents plus...". And you thought math was boring!

I'm hoping that someday I have money to burn. I'm dying to call up and order a pizza one day, and tell them it's for an eccentric relative who has a doctorate in mathematics from MIT. He refuses to eat pizza that's unevenly cut, but he tips handsomely for well-cut pizza. Then when I place the order, I tell the guy I need it cut into 17 equal pieces, but for the extra effort, I'm willing to tip $500. A lot of the fun may be wasted by the fact that I won't be able to see them going ape shit trying to meet the challenge. But just knowing they are could have some value. While you're at it, tell them you want a fountain Diet Coke, but it has to match the patented formula exactly. Then tell them you have a gas chromatograph to make sure they don't cheat. Guaranteed, at least one person working that night will leave the shop in a straight jacket.

ASSAULT ON PEPPER

I don't like peppers. Green peppers, red peppers, yellow peppers, bell peppers, hot peppers, cold peppers, pickled peppers. I hate them all. Is it so difficult for people to keep them the fuck out of my food?? I don't want them on my pizza. I don't want them on my salad. I don't want them fucking anywhere!

And don't even give me that shit about "well, just pick them off/out". Fuck you! Don't put them on in the first fucking place!! This may be something you can't get through that thick skull of yours, but I'll try to spell it out for you. All peppers, no matter what kind, secrete fluid. If you take a cut pepper, put it in a glass of water, leave it there for a half hour then take it out, and taste the water, it will taste like fucking peppers! You can't see it in the water, but you can smell it and taste it. That same effect occurs when it's on any of my food. If you put peppers on my salad, it won't take long for the invisible fluid to infect the lettuce, tomato, and whatever else happens to be on there. Even if I pick the peppers off, the damage has been done! I might as well give the fucking salad to the dog! If you like peppers, fine. Put them on your food, but keep them the fuck off of mine!

Next person who gives me food with peppers on it and tells me to pick them off, I'm going to grab their food and take a shit on it. Then I'll tell them "*just pick it off*"!

AN ORIGINAL TOPIC

I handle a lot of legal documents at my job. On many occasions, the customer will want documents submitted to them in duplicate, triplicate or fourplicate (whatever the hell that's really called). However, sometimes they'll want the original and the copies to be distinguishable by labeling them "Original" and "Copy". This to me is a pointless endeavor. If you take the original, label it "Original" then make copies, all the copies will say "Original". On the other hand, if you take the original, make copies, **then** label the original as "Original", then the copies cease to be true copies because the original was altered! I guess some companies have special paper that says "Original" on it, but when used on a photocopier the "Original" label doesn't show up. Well, guess what? My company doesn't have that. How about this? Next time I need to label something "Original", I'll masturbate all over it, then send it. You'll be able to distinguish the original by the fact that the pages all stick together. Satisfied??

TWO VERY POOR JOKES

A black guy got busted for soliciting the services of a prostitute. How it all started was from a call he made to the police when he was witnessing a woman getting mugged and assaulted. When the police finally arrived, the mugger was long gone. He yelled at the officer "Cop, you late"! The officer thought he said 'copulate' and took him into custody.

What does spicy rice with andouille sausage and shrimp in it, and a big, fat person who can't tell the truth have in common? They're both "jumbo liar" (jambalaya)!

This is the reason I don't write many traditional jokes.

THEIR, THEIR

I've been pushing, for a long time, to make "they" and "their" singular, gender-independent terms. You can go to any grammar book and it will tell you that's an incorrect use, but I think it's time to change that. Here's an example. When you're referring to a position that could be held by either a man or woman, proper grammar said to account for it by using "his/hers", "he/she", etc. A couple of proper sentence samples would be "In case of fire, the company president should pull down his/her pants and urinate on the blaze. Afterward, he/she shall put his/her pants back on and return to work". Is this not the clumsiest, most awkward grammar in the English language?? Wouldn't it be so much smoother and easier to be able to say "Afterward, **they** shall put **their** pants back on and return to work"? See how nicely that rolls off the tongue?

A funny thing though. Just recently I read a document that simply used "He" in place of "He/She". Doesn't this indicate some kind of regression in gender rights. What the hell is next? Forbidding women from voting??

COKE HEADS

I enjoy Coca-Cola. I especially like when it comes from the fountain rather than from the can or bottle. But I have a question. Since the two have a distinctively different taste, which one is the intended taste? Coke apparently has this trillion-dollar formula they have been using for decades. It's kept under higher security than smallpox at the CDC in Atlanta. But by process of elimination, only one of the Cokes (either the fountain or the can/bottle) can be the real Coke. And if that's true, then one must be a hoax. Think about that. Everyday, people drink thousands, millions of Coca-Colas. Part of them come in cans and bottles and the other part are dispensed from soda fountains. And one of them is fake! Millions of people everyday think they're drinking the real Coke and they're being duped! People are easy to fool apparently. At least Coke drinkers.

SUCK IT UP

Hooters is a restaurant chain known for its great food. Hah!! That's a good one! It's fairly common knowledge that, in fact, they're famous for having hookers...err...I mean, waitresses with big tits. I have another great idea. Come out with a similar food chain and call it "Hoovers". The catch is that all the waitresses give awesome blow jobs. Actually, that probably holds true for the Hooters girls. They just don't advertise it as openly as the tit thing.

PROSTITUTORS

I don't agree with the fact that prostitution is illegal in almost every state. I think the government is missing out on huge taxation and licensing opportunities myself. But for those of you who live outside of Las Vegas and have the need (by choice or by design) to pay for sex rather than just begging for it like the rest of us, here's a way you can protect yourself (and your would-be rented lover) from legal repercussions. Carry around a small notebook with "2 + 2 = ??" written in it. After the sexual shenanigans, open the book and ask her if she can help you answer that equation. When she (hopefully!) tells you the answer is "4", you can pay her as a tutor, with the sex being incidental. Granted you can probably get tutoring at a far better price, but most tutors won't throw in an *around-the-world* as a bonus.

JABBA THE SLUT

There's nothing that pisses me off quite as bad as a slender, good-looking woman walking around with a big, fat fucking pig of a man. I do have a theory about how these lopsided couples come to exist. It's my hypothesis that these fat, ugly bastards go to parties that have lots of hot women, wait for them to get drunk (enough so that their judgment is severely impaired) and then get them to go to bed with them, or more likely, wait for them to pass out. At that point, they have sex with them and get them pregnant. Then it's just a matter of luck whether or not the woman will have an abortion or have the child and stay with the walking garbage bag filled with cottage cheese out of a dedication to and for the sake of her child. Ladies, everyone makes mistakes. You can do better. There's no need to ruin your entire lives for one night of indiscretion. This message is a public service, brought to you by The Awful Show.

I HAD A DREAM I WAS EATING A SHEEP...

I was looking at the tag on a pillow the other day. You know those infamous tags they put on mattresses and bedding and stuff that have something like "It's against the law to remove this tag! If you remove it, the sleep police will hunt you down and imprison you for life where you'll be anal raped nightly by a large, smelly, HIV-positive inmate...". Well, they don't actually say anything like that, but you get the idea of the overblown infamy of these tags. Anyway, the wording was actually more something along the line of "*It is unlawful for this tag to be removed by anyone but the consumer*". That gave me a weird feeling all of a sudden. Is 'consumer' the word they really meant there. Is the tag implying that the proper use of a pillow is to eat it?? I know that consumer has a different more generalized meaning, but still the word is just weird. Oh, well. That's something to chew on I guess.

REPEAT AFTER ME

Music will always be one aspect of pop culture rife with criticizable aspects. Two of these aspects center on rhyming. First of all, I have no tolerance anymore for worn out rhyme schemes. There are a few in particular I would like to address now.

HEART-START-APART
This selection of words has been worn out for a very, **very** long time! There's a song most people know (and that makes about as many sick) called "*Don't Go Breaking My Heart*". It was by Elton John and was done as a duet with Kiki Dee in 1976 and again with RuPaul in 1993 (As much temptation as I have right now to make never-ending fun of RuPaul teaming up with Elton John, I shall try to stay on topic). The lyrics at one point go "*Right from the start, I gave you my heart*". Back in the 1970s, this was acceptable. Music was generally lame back then anyway. It fit the genre well. But it wasn't in any way, shape, or form what can be considered 'cool'. Just as it was also not cool in the 1990s (I would call it kitschy, considering it was a remake). So if it wasn't cool then, why the hell do any of these musical "artists" (term used loosely) think it's going to be cool now?? If you absolutely need to include the -art rhyme in your song somewhere, consider using 'fart'. That may not be cool either, but at least there's a humor element. And what the hell is it with the heart anyway? It's a blood-pumping organ. It isn't the center of all loving emotion. In fact, if you ever saw an actual heart up close, enough so that you could touch the squishy vascular tissue, it

would probably at least make you gag. How the fuck is **that** romantic?!? Okay, that's enough of that one.

GLAD-BAD-SAD-MAD

This is my next loathed literary abomination. It's just straight-up nursery rhyme shit. If you're planning on writing a song, and anywhere in it you have any of these words forming a rhyme at the end of a sentence, just stop. Crumple up the paper and start over. This belongs in children's book, not music. Unless it's children's music. Again, a recommendation: if you feel the all-consuming, uncontrollable need to include any of these words at the end of a line and are looking for a rhyme, consider using 'maxi-pad'.

There are other atrocities I can mention, but for now I want to move on to the other major problem with rhyming: Using the same word to rhyme with itself. This is about the most obvious indication that the person singing has less talent in them than a stuttering 4-year-old in a Christmas pageant. Two of the ones that immediately spring to my mind are John Mellencamp and Kanye West. Right there, it's plain to see that there's no particular era of music this is akin to. It's an epidemic as old as singing itself probably. John Mellencamp is a particular stand out because of his song "Small Town". Here are some statistics. There are a total of 29 individual lines in the song. Of them, the phrase "small town" falls at the end of 16 of them. That's over 55% of the song all ending with the same goddamn term!! How is this music?? It's repetition; nothing more! I half expect one of the fucking lines to just be "Small town, small town, small town, small town"! As if that weren't bad enough, of the remaining 13 line of the song, 5 of the lines end with the word 'me'. More fucking repetition! And just as the clincher that this long-haired hillbilly fuck has no lyric-writing talent at all, 2 of the remaining 8 lines end with "big town". Who the fuck didn't see that coming!!

Enough already with John Menstrualcramp. The other target for this discussion is the ultimate talentless jackoff himself, Kayne West. While his repetition doesn't come close to Mellencamp's (with a song like "Small Town", who the fuck could??), his part in the Keri Hilson song "Knock You Down" is a much more efficient slap in the face of people who actually pay for his shit. Here's the big pair of lines: "This is bad, real bad, Michael Jackson. Now I'm mad, real mad, Joe Jackson". Where to fucking start with this turd...?? First of all, as I mentioned before, rhyming "bad" with "mad"...total Mother Goose horseshit. I can just imagine Miss Molly from Romper Room reading Kayne West "poetry" to all the little bastards she sees in that magic mirror of hers. That was bad enough. Unfortunate enough, should I say. I feel dirty using the word 'bad' at the moment. The other part of the amateur nature of this is rhyming Jackson with Jackson. Is it starting to become abundantly clear that this fucking loser has no talent at all?? Just like Mellencamp, what's the next line "Jackson, Jackson, Jackson, Jackson, Jackson"?!? *Hey, look everyone! I can rhyme just like Kanye! Give me a million dollars!*

So to add some sort of closure to this. If you're an aspiring songwriter, please take your time and choose your rhymes much more carefully than the aforementioned hacks. And for Christ's sake, if you're having difficulty coming up with unique rhymes, do everyone a favor and buy a rhyming dictionary at the bookstore. I, and the rest of the music-listening country, thank you.

Oh, and before I forget, take a good long time to think about your band name. Have you seen some of the names in modern music? The Goo-Goo Dolls? Lady Gaga? When the fuck did it become customary to take naming cues from someone who isn't even a month old? I can only imagine how successful The Beatles would have been if they were named The Ca-Ca Poo-Poo Band.

THAT'LL LEARN YA

I can't expect that the South will ever catch up to the North in their ability to speak intelligently. But let me just ask one thing. Did you ever hear a guy say "*My daddy didn't raise no fool*"? I would love to think that I'm the only one who hears this and feels like someone just took a metal fork and scrapped it down a chalkboard. I kind of doubt that's the case though. In a situation like this, I feel the need to come back with "*Be that as it may, he also didn't raise anyone with a grasp of the English language, you fucking hick*"! Let's all make a pact. Next time you hear this, grab a pitchfork off of the guy's pick-up and jam it right into his nuts. Maybe that will prevent him from breeding any further. Of course if he's older than 11, it's probably too late.

IN THE PINK

Women have the gift of ever being able to fuck with the minds of men. Especially when it comes to homosexuality.

What really got me thinking of this was the singer Pink. I think her real name is Alecia Beth Moore. Anyway, if you haven't seen her, she's this spikey-haired, very butch-looking female who is apparently straight. Looking at this woman, the first thought that would cross any man's mind is 'dyke'! But in fact she's married (or was at one time) to a guy by the name of Carey Hart.

Then take a look at a woman like Ellen DeGeneres. A full-blown confirmed carpet-muncher. However, very feminine in appearance. She has in fact played a straight woman in many movies, and quite convincingly at that! And if you look at her partner, Portia de Rossi, you'll see an even-more feminine and sexy woman!

Men on the other hand are easy to spot. If they mince around and have that little half-lisp, they're queer. If they don't they probably aren't.

I don't know if this is some kind of trick that nature is playing on us men, but it isn't fucking funny. Maybe someday there'll be a clear physical sign of sexuality, like a birthmark or something. That's going to make bar-hopping so much easier when it happens.

WHAT DID THAT WAITER JUST CALL ME?!?

This is either one of my most brilliant money-venture ideas, or one of my worst. You can decide.

A while ago, on one of those lesser cable networks (You know, the kind that needs to be packaged in with a bunch of other ones because no one would ever pay for the channel by itself) I saw a show that went to various restaurants around the country and tried to find the weirdest or quirkiest ones around. One memorable one was a hot dog stand that was run by 3 rather large black women. Their gimmick was, quite simply, treating the customers like shit. Not like spitting in their food, but just being monumentally rude, swearing at them and insulting them at every turn. This got me thinking on a new restaurant idea of my own...

The idea was to come up with a list of all the different racial stereotypes as they associate to food. You would then proceed to make a menu with the most offensive names for the different meals as possible. "The Nigger Plate" would be fried chicken and collard greens with watermelon. You could come up with a collection of kosher foods for the "Kike's Delight". Naturally an assortment of Mexican foods would be offered as "The Wetback Platter".

While I'm sure that the restaurant would do well enough, it might be excessively difficult getting insurance considering all the fist fights that would be likely to break out just from people ordering.

I DIDN'T DO NOTHIN'!

There are some words in the English language that need to be completely done away with. I'm not talking about profane words or racial slurs or anything like that. I'm talking about words that are just fucking pointless.

One such word is "Allegedly". Whenever you listen to the news, keep a notepad and pencil handy. Pick any half-hour news cast and keep track of how many times the newscaster uses the word 'allegedly'. Don't be surprised to find the count somewhere in the 40s at the end of 30 minutes.

I can understand the thought behind it. There's probably some legal precedent that requires people in the media to protect their interests by not stating certain things as fact when an investigation is ongoing or what have you. But when you can't get through a 2-minute story without using the word 'allegedly' a half dozen times, it's time to rethink the way we present this shit.

But one of the big reasons 'allegedly' needs to be done away with is the range of its use. Unless the person speaking was actually a witness to whatever they're talking about, they can use 'allegedly' in every fucking sentence! And if the person who is listening to the account goes and tells someone else, they can use it even more! Does this not strike anyone else as the most fucking ridiculous and pointless terminologies in the language??

I think people just need to start showing some fucking backbone and taking a stand. If you say something that later turns out to be wrong, send out a retraction. Or do a follow-up story that clarifies and corrects the old one. But whatever you do, stop fucking saying 'allegedly'! If I have to keep hearing this word, I'm going to hunt down all the offending newscasters and pull their genitals over their shoes!! Allegedly.

THE RETURN OF THOUGHTS THAT ARE TOO SHORT FOR THEIR OWN SECTIONS IN THIS BOOK EVEN THOUGH THE TITLE IS ALMOST A PARAGRAPH ITSELF

- I love the concept of the coconut bra. Pina Colada-flavored titties.
- Here's a phrase I don't like: "Feeling someone out"? I guess in popular usage, it means to get an idea of a person's perspective or viewpoint on a particular issue. It sounds much dirtier though. Compare it to the phrase "feeling someone up" and you'll see what I mean. Better wear a glove!
- Death is the cure for cancer (Wow! **That** was fucking dark)!!
- A punchline without a joke: ...and the second gynecologist says "Fundus? We're lucky she doesn't sue us"!
- You know a term that doesn't quite seem appropriate. *Cocktail sauce.* When I think of cocktails, I think of fruity drinks with umbrellas. If I ever get a drink served to me that tastes like ketchup and horseradish, I'm kicking the bartender's ass!
- One of the reasons I hate clichés: "Good things come to those who wait", but "he who hesitates has lost". **Ahhhhhhhhh!!!!**
- Pop music has the greatest scam going. Remixes. Nowadays, an artist can take a song they have already done, tweak the music a little, and sell it off like it's a brand-new song. I'm glad file-sharing is killing the industry. Those motherfuckers don't deserve money for that shit.

- Here's a great idea for a new series. "Solid Gold 2010". The catch is you bring back all the original dancers and make them wear the same outfits. Naturally you would need to put it on the SciFi Channel because it would most likely be pretty horrifying. Plus you never know when one of them is going to fall and break a hip.
- Wouldn't it be cool if there was a wide receiver in the NFL who was really good, but he involuntarily threw up after every touchdown? And they showed it on TV? I think not only would people become desensitized to it, but it might just catch on as a fad. There would be one copycat on every team. It would certainly make eating chips and salsa during the game interesting.
- When driving on the interstate or some other major road, have you seen trucks driving around with "Peterbilt" on them? I am all for creative means of manufacturing, but I'm not totally comfortable either driving or being near a vehicle someone put together with his dick.
- Lots of people say, "violence is not the answer". But what if the question is "What word does Merriam-Webster define as [exertion of physical force so as to injure or abuse]"? So much for all the touchy-feely pacifist bullshit!
- I don't think I would necessarily want to give looks that could kill. I think it would be more fun to be able to give looks that maim.
- Is cannibalism a requisite when one is hungry for baby-back ribs?

- Hyundai is simply a gross mispronunciation of the name Honda. In actuality, they're the same rice-burner piece of shit.
- I wonder how many gallons of blood are expelled vaginally on a daily basis due to menstruation. And then I vomit.
- Does the guy who fills the RC Cola machine aspire to fill the Coke machine someday? Is there jealousy?
- I saw a sign that said "Watch Children". I admit. Keeping an eye on them does make them easier to hit with my car.

HOT TOPIC THE 13TH

After seeing the latest *Friday the 13th* remake, I think I have an idea to end the series for good. Make all the camp counselors suicidal emo kids. Every time Jason attacked one, they wouldn't run. They just stand there waiting to be killed. By the fifth one, Jason would be so frustrated, he'd be handing them weapons, turning them around and pushing them so they'd run away. Anything to make it a little more sporting. By the end of the movie Jason is so depressed that he, with a little fancy machete work, cuts his own head off. I think I would actually pay to see that in the theater.

PUT YOUR MONEY WHERE MY MOUTH IS!

As I've said in the past I despise people who file these frivolous lawsuits, but I think the real reason for that is jealousy. I don't have a lawyer at my beck and call like some do. But I do have some pretty good ideas from time to time.

Take these places that make claims to having the world's best coffee, the world's hottest wings, etc. Think about the use of these superlatives. If you have been around, you know that there are plenty of places making identical claims. But by process of elimination, only one place, at most, can be truthful in their claim. Everyone else is engaged in false advertising.

So here's my idea. For any claim, hold a contest. Let's say we're doing one for "the world's best coffee". There are no shortage of cafés, restaurants, and even gas stations making that claim. Invite them all to a big coffee-off. Have it held in some central U.S. location to make it easier for anyone nationwide to attend. Also, invite coffee aficionados and in general anyone who enjoys coffee on a regular basis, just to have a truly democratic and diverse collection of "judges". All of the participants bring their best and offer samples. Once everyone has had a chance to sample all the different attendants offerings, they rate their top 3. Once all the ballots are collected and tabulated, a winner is declared and a class action suit filed against everyone else who lost. The details of the class action suit involve a settlement going to every coffee customer who has ever patronized said losers.

Nothing like a billion-dollar lawsuit to make those fuckers take down those "World's Best" signs!

GO TO HELL, IF THEY HAVE ANY VACANCIES

No matter how bad things may get, there's always suicide.

I can only imagine the look on the faces of people who just read that! HAHAHAHAH!! Okay, anyway. That was really just a statement to lead into my next religion bashing. This one is generally aimed at the Catholics.

It's my understanding that Catholics believe that anyone who commits suicide will go to hell. I don't have a problem with that in light of all the other ridiculous shit they spout off about. What I'm having a problem with is the whole "hell" thing. I think it's generally thought and agreed upon that, directionally speaking, Heaven is up and hell is down. Now let's examine the real estate involved with this philosophy.

Up leads away from the planet, or in other words, off into the infinite vastness of space. There's no shortage of elbow room when it comes to that! Billions and billions of cubic light-years to be precise. Well, in a manner of speaking. There's a lot of fucking space, okay?? That's why it's called *space*! Now, what about hell? Hell is down, into the earth. But there's a fatal flaw here. You can only go so far down before you're going back up on the other side. Since the earth is a finite mass, hell must have a limited area it can occupy. At some point hell would have to run out of room. And considering the millions of people who have committed suicide since the dawn of man, it has got to be getting pretty close to maximum sinner capacity. And that's not yet even including all the people who are in hell for other reasons! What exactly is hell's capacity? Is there any mention of this in the bible?

The whole thing just reeks of outdated and illogical thought. I'm sure one day, some clergyman will concoct answers to these questions, but I've already lost interest in hearing what they are. Fuck hell!

(I) MEAN (,) PEOPLE SUCK!

This planet would be a great place to live if it weren't for all the fucking humans. Think about that. If all the humans disappeared, you would be left with animals, plants, and microbes. To say it would be a peaceful place wouldn't be entirely accurate, but such is animal life. Yet, the only violence that would occur would be for the sake of survival. Maybe a little territorial scuffling, but generally the only time animals would be looking to kill one another, it's pretty much so someone can eat. Likewise, they don't *think* about killing. They don't ponder things like "*That fucking gazelle is pissing me off! Tonight, when he's drinking from the river, I'm going to kill him*"! Just about everything they do comes from an instinct, an unconscious drive.

That isn't to say that animals don't have emotions. If you take a little 3-pound kitten, and in front of it you put a 400-pound Rottweiler, that kitten will be scared shitless. It will turn itself inside-out with its head going directly back and right out of its anus trying to get the fuck out of there! And even that is partially attributed to instinct as it relates to fight or flight. The kitten doesn't consciously sit there and think "Hey! That's a big motherfucker! That beast might be looking to turn me into a snack. I think its best that I take a very quick shit at this very spot, then get the fuck out of here"! And the kitten is gone. So most everything these animals do comes down to instinct.

And while a planet without humans may be primitive, at least there wouldn't be people like Kenneth Lay and Bernie Madoff shitting in the punch bowl.

AN OMNI-RACIAL SLUR??

I'm no stranger to the power of racial slurs. Nothing gets a fist fight going faster! But there have been several times I've wanted to use a racial slur, but unfortunately didn't know which one to use. Here's what I mean.

Have you ever talked to someone in Tech Support. And naturally they're an American and they're talking to you from America. **HAHAHHAHAHAHHAAA!!** Oh, that was a good one! Almost pissed myself laughing with that one. No, seriously. Why would anyone use Americans for tech support. I mean, shit! You would actually have to pay them more than 45 cents an hour! So here you are on the phone with one of these foreign fucks, and they all sound like Apu from *The Simpsons*. The problem is you can't tell if they're from India, Pakistan, Outer Mongolia...you don't have a fucking clue where this smelly harem spawn is! And you know the worthless motherfucker either has pissed you off with their incompetence or will in the near future. So you get steamed up and you say "Hey! Listen you...uhhh..." and you're reaching for a racial slur, but you have no idea which one to use! It's frustrating!

It's because of situations like this that I've come up with the perfect solution. The word is "ghint" (pronounced "*gint*"). 'Ghint' is a generic racial slur. It doesn't matter if you're talking to someone in the Middle East, in Asia, or even in America. 'Ghint' is a term you can use with any race to attack their ethnicity on a personal and hurtful level. It contains all of the emotion of a racial slur without actually specifying a race. This can be especially useful when you're speaking to someone who is of mixed ethnicity. Kind of like a little of everything, like the bi-product of a Benetton orgy. Another great use is when you're talking to someone who is the same race as you. If I'm chewing out a white guy and I use the term 'honky', it doesn't have much punch to it since it's coming *from* a honky. However, by whipping out the term 'ghint', the emotional level is raised a few notches. Same goes for if you're Italian and you're going toe to toe with another Italian. You can call him a guinea wop dago until the French bread pizza dings, but it isn't going to nearly mean as much coming from you as 'ghint' will. For the record, I was married to an Italian for 5 years, so I've earned the right to use that earlier terminology.

Yet another use is when you're dealing with a race that simply doesn't have a good strong racial slur associated with them to begin with. Like what do you call someone from Pago Pago? Whatever you call them, it's probably pretty fucking weak. Using 'ghint', as Emeril Lagasse would say, kicks it up a notch. By the way, Emeril is a blend of French-Canadian and Portuguese; a perfect example of when to use 'ghint'!

I've come up with some other good terms lately, not just revolving around racial hatred. One of my more recent ones was 'bitch pipe'. When it first fell out of my mouth, it was a little stunning. You'd think I would be accustomed to my pseudo-Tourette's verbal spasms by now, but strangely I'm still capable of throwing myself for a loop now and then. It was important enough though to at least consider giving it a definition. And the conclusion I came to is that a bitch pipe is another term for a vagina. I had to consider a few options before deciding on this. Naturally, the 'pipe' part could have represented any orifice. Mouth, anus, vagina, urethra, ear canal, nostril, whatever. Any place on the body that could conceivably be a receptacle for a dick, or at the very least an ejaculation. Then 'bitch' would imply woman. Wait. Wait! Whoa! Hold it, ladies! Before you attack, I didn't say 'woman implies bitch'! Don't get your Kotex in a knot. What I mean is that the only orifice specific to the woman is the vagina. So there you have it. 'Bitch pipe' means vagina. So guys, the next time you want to put your man pole in something, put it in her bitch pipe!

So that's all I have to say about that, ya ghint bitch pipes!

BE A MAN!

There is without a doubt an unwritten book of man laws. Miller Lite made a commercial about them some time back with Triple H and Jerome Bettis. I think Burt Reynolds was in there too. But it's true, there are indeed a set of rules for dudes called 'man laws'. I've even come up with a few myself if a book is ever really written.

Most of the truly horrific man rules are unsurprisingly experienced in high school; the first frontier of masculinity. The first man rule was applicable to guys who didn't use backpacks. Over the past dozen or so years, backpacks have increased in popularity, with people having to carry all their iPods and laptops and cell phones and Blackberrys and shit. Also when we got to college those who hadn't already done so graduated to backpacks. There really wasn't much of a choice for students like myself who consistently carried 16 credits. No one has long enough fingers to hand-carry that many books. Even with this new storage and transport accessory, we were little more than pack mules, carrying a bag loaded with 75 pounds of hardbacks in it from class to class. In retrospect it's kind of surprising more students didn't graduate inflicted with a case of backpack-induced scoliosis.

But when it came to high school, back in the day, we carried our books by hand. And there was only one way to do it: at your side with your arm straight and your fingers wrapped around the side of the books. When the girls carried their books, they did it the logical way by contrast. This was either done with one or two hands and the books were held more upright with the bottoms resting against the female's side or just under her tits and the whole forearm around the back of the books. But that was the *girls'* way of carrying them. Guys were not allowed to do it this way. The reason being 'because'. This was the basis for all Man Laws; the almighty 'because'. Guys, at all times, had to carry their books the *'man way'*. This made it all that much easier for Billy Cocksmoke and Tommy Nosack to sneak up from behind and shove the books right out of your hand and all over the floor. And as if this wasn't bad enough, all of the homework that was folded an placed inside the book would go flying out in another dozen or so directions. Why was the homework folded and placed inside the book instead of being kept organized in a folder? Guess. Man law. This was made all the worse by the fact that no one in high school can resist the temptation to step on anything on the floor that happens to be unsoiled. Be it your homework or a brand new pair of sneakers, the bottom of a teenager's shoes are magnetically attracted to anything clean and white.

There was a little influence from nature involved in the spilling of homework too. When it was sunny and warm out, spills were much less likely to occur than when it was rainy or snowy out. This is because when the weather was (as the editorializing weatherman would say) "pleasant", the hallways weren't rife with dirty water and slush from people tracking it in and making the floor little more than a cross between a swamp and an aqueduct. I never quite figured that out, but I suspect it had to do with the molecular attraction of water molecules we were told about in third period. Whether that was the reason or not, the end result was the same: Your homework ended up looking like something Frosty the Snowman wiped his ass with.

So there you have yet another example of the stupidity of men, wrapped in the cosmic container dubbed "Man Law". So it is (un)written, so shall it be done. And if it does get written, it will be knocked on the floor and stepped on.

GENTLEMEN, START YOUR PECKERS!

This is another one that's just for the guys. As will be apparent in about 2 seconds. Did you ever have to pull-start your cock? That may sound strange but let me explain what I mean.

Say you're outside and it's bitter cold. The temperature is somewhere between 'witch's tit' and 'penguin sack'. You might be shoveling snow or even just out sledding. You're wearing tight jeans at the time, because you no longer fit in that snow suit you wore in second grade. Naturally, a time rolls around where you have to take a piss after the gallon and a half of hot chocolate you consumed is done being processed. You go inside, unzip your pants and go to grab your cock. Much to your dismay, your tool isn't there! No, I don't mean it's totally gone! It's there, but it just so happens that penises don't like the cold. They like it much better inside the warm toastiness of the area inside your pelvis. All that's left on the outside is hair and a mushroom top. At this point, you have a choice. You can either try to piss with your member retracted, taking a chance of getting urine all over yourself, or the more logical method, grab the head and pull. If you have ever done the latter, you have *pull-started* your cock. Isn't it nice to learn something about your body you didn't realize?

SOUP'S ON (FIRE)

On a soup and salad buffet, why do they keep the temperature of the soup just slightly below that of molten lava? I think I have a guess. I believe it's a strategy of the restaurant to save money.

If the restaurants keep the soup at a hot but eatable temperature, people would go back for seconds and thirds a lot more than they do having to wait 30 minutes for the first bowl to cool down enough to put the spoon in without it melting.

You know what I say? Fuck it! I still eat the shit! I don't care if I have those flesh stalagmites hanging down from the roof of my mouth for a week. I'm not letting the establishment try to fuck me out of *all-I-can-eat*! Ahh, there's that Y-chromosome again!

OH, KEYZ!

Quite recently on the show, I started doing a segment called "*Oh, Keyz*"! It's really simply a brief bit (usually under a minute in length) of something I found interesting, disturbing or infuriating. Almost like a personal commercial of editorialization. I'm going to close out this book with a collection of those. Some I've used, some I may use in the future, and some I may realize are too dumb to use. But if the lattest is the case, I at least want them here in writing. Plus, if I weeded out all the "potentially stupid" material from this book, it would probably have ended up just slightly thicker than a pamphlet! And now it's time for another episode of "*Oh, Keyz*"!

There's a song called "Birthday Sex". What a great idea this is! It used to be that you wanted toys or clothes. Now you're just happy to get laid!

Remember the 1980's "Lean on Me" remake. Jesus Christ, did that suck! What was wrong with the original?? I think these fucking "artists" need to try doing remakes of shitty songs. That would make a lot more sense. Do-over!

Women don't have it as hard as they like to think. Take the bar scene. If they so much as flash a tit, they'll have guys buying drinks for them all night. If I tried that with my man boobs, I'd be liable to get shot!

Here's a great tattoo idea! Have a tattoo that says "Not Dead". But have the "Not" done in hypercolor ink. That way, when the body temperature drops after death, the "Not" will fade away leaving just "Dead". Then people don't have to waste time looking for a pulse!

Here's a leftover question from the show's version of The Match Game (dubbed *'Snatch Game'*). "Freaky Frieda is so freaky...she had surgery on her beaver. Now it actually has (blank)." There would be some great answers people could come up with. Buck teeth would probably be the most painful.

There is surgery to make lips bigger. Have you noticed though never hear about surgery to make nostrils wider. That there is what I call *subtle* racism.

I want to get political for a moment. I think we need to forget about Iraq and Pakistan. What we need to attack is Nigeria! You would be doing the world a great service. After all, that's where all those internet scams come from! Why fight regular terrorism when e-terrorism is so much wider spread??

There was an actual band a while ago named *The Povertyneck Hillbillies*. Exactly how much further can a band go to insulting themselves? I can just imagine hearing of a band named *The Inbred Shit-Eating Retards*.

Whenever you hear about Santa Claus, you occasionally hear of Mrs. Claus. I'm waiting to hear about Mistress Clause. Some slender woman with huge tits in a red PVC catsuit with a long whip. Merry fucking Christmas!

Whenever you live in an apartment building and you see someone has received a package but hasn't taken it into their place yet, don't you get sad that it isn't for you or that you didn't get one too? What are we? 6 years old??

Joe Pesci, in "Easy Money" said, "*Men don't have style. Men wear clothes. Women have style*". That hits the nail right on the head as far as my sense of fashion. The big trend now seems to be these jeans that are worn-out looking. I don't think it's an appearance though. I think these designers are going to Goodwill and buying worn out jeans by the truckload then putting their nametags on them and selling them as new. I know times are tough, but have some fucking scruples will ya?

My personal solution to the homeless. Don't give them money. Give them camping equipment. As far as I'm concerned I would much rather find a nice little area in the woods and hunt and fish for survival as opposed to sitting on a street corner waiting for a handout. The cities are crowded; there's plenty of uninhabited woods though. And if they're alcoholics, download and print out an article on making moonshine for them.

Since broadcasting has now gone totally digital, does that mean the airwaves are free for pirate television stations? It should be. Then maybe there'd be something good on to watch!

You know something that's never drawn realistically? Snowmen. Every time you see a drawing of a snowman, they're pristine white. When you see one in real life, they're loaded with all kinds of leaves and grass clippings stuck in them. Come on, artists! Get with the program!

Here's a number you never hear anyone use: A dozen hundred. Why not? It's a legitimate number; one thousand, two hundred. I need to find a use for that more often. If for no other reason than confusing the shit out of people.

In my industry, we have a thing called liquidated damages. Whenever we ship a product late, we have to pay the customer back a certain amount daily for every day we're late. This would be a great idea for doctors! When the doctor keeps the patient waiting, they have to pay the patient for every minute that passes after the appointment time. Maybe that will get those lazy, overpaid fucks on the ball!

Here's a word no one uses: constipates. It's a real word. When something blocks you up, it constipates you. Instead of saying "Cheese makes me constipated", simply say "Cheese *constipates* me". Try to work it into your daily life.

I love when I have **big** stretches. Like whole body stretches. Toes, nostrils, everything! Funny thing about me though. When I do those, my groin pops. I know that sounds dirty, but I don't mean it in "that way". I mean there's a popping feeling in my lower abdomen. It doesn't hurt or anything, but it bothers me because I would just like to know what the fuck it is!

How are blind people attracted to others? I can't figure this out. People say that attraction, even though it shouldn't be, is based on looks. If you can't see someone though, what replaces that? I would think pussy or dick smell would have a much higher bearing in some way.

I don't believe in god, but even if I did, I wouldn't worship him. Or her. It! The reason being: I'm getting little beards growing out of my nose and ears. Is that supposed to be some kind of joke? Guess what, dick! It isn't fucking funny!

Here's another great tip for being a pain in the ass. Whenever someone advertises something as "Ice Cold" carry a thermometer around and check the temperature. If it isn't 32 degrees Fahrenheit or less, demand your money back or you're going to sue them for false advertising.

As if anyone needs another sign that society is going to shit. Remember when people use to write, "wash me" with their finger on really dirty cars. I recently saw a dirty car in a parking lot with writing that said, "Clean your fucking car, asshole"! I can only see what's coming next. Instead of kids putting signs that say, "Kick me" on other kids' backs, the sign will read "Shove a table lamp up my ass"!

If there was this brand-new street drug that gave this amazing euphoric feeling and that made you love everyone and everything and there was no chemical addiction, side effects or hangover from it, but the only way to take it was injecting it directly into your eyeball with a syringe, do you think people would still do it? I think they would. Sick fuckers!

When it comes to Christmas music, it isn't so much the forced religion of it that gets me. It's simply that it's the type of music that sticks in your head for about a decade! If Bing Crosby wasn't already dead, I would kill the motherfucker!

I'm sick of these rappers using 'rock' in their lyrics as if that's what their 'music' was. Pay attention, assholes! It isn't rock. It's rap. Okay? Run-DMC says "I'm the king of rock..." No! Bullshit! You may be the king of rap, arguably. But unless you have 2 guys playing some form of guitar with real strings and a drum set that isn't on a microchip, it isn't fucking rock!

Did you ever get stuck working with a guy who says "I don't want a gay guy working with me. He'll be hitting on me and trying to get me in bed all the time". Now you know what the **women** fell like, fuckhead!!

Listening to music from back in the 60s and 70s now that I'm older is quite an enlightening experience. Like the song "Afternoon Delight". When I was a kid, I had no idea what it was about. I thought it was some sort of ice cream treat! I never fathomed that it was about some guy coming home for lunch and sticking his dick in a woman!

Here's something I'm getting sick of. Every time I go to get my oil changed, they tell me I have to rotate my tires. I always just laugh them off. What do they think I'm stupid? They're just trying to milk me for more money. For Christ's sake, every time I drive the car, the tires rotate! Okay, I'm not actually that automotively ignorant. I just thought it was funny.

When I'm in traffic, I sometimes see the little compact SUV (oxymoron alert) from Suzuki. It's the XL-7. But on the spare tire cover, instead of a dash they use an underscore. Now **that's** some cool-ass, modern-day shit! The only thing cooler than that would have been if they used a backslash.

My medium-low level of racism is fairly well known, but I think I leveled up a while back. When I was visiting a friend in the hospital, in the gift shop window there was a ceramic angel that was black. To which I said: "Oh, please! Like a black person would ever go to heaven"! I guess people should just start calling me Keyz Hitler. While I'm being a total redneck, I don't like when people refer to Barack Obama as being half-black. I say, fuck that! He's just black! Okay? If you make a milkshake and take one scoop of vanilla ice cream and one scoop of shit and blend it, what's it going to taste like? Would you say "This milkshake tastes like half shit"? Fuck no! You would say "This milkshake tastes like shit"! I think I may be Grand Dragon material. Sad.

Don't you love when you drive by a Subway restaurant while

they're hiring and the sign reads, "Come join our sandwich artist team"? How brainless do these fuckers think people are? Sandwich artist? Bullshit! You're a sandwich maker. Unless you're recreating the Mona Lisa with pastrami and mustard, you're just a fucking minimum wage, Ford-Escort-driving sandwich maker!

Isn't it strange that we have volunteer fire fighters but we don't have volunteer police? If there were, I would have volunteered a long time ago. I'd be giving a whole new meaning to police brutality!

I think there needs to be a car company that makes unconventionally-named models. Like "The Shitbox" or "The Douche Bucket". Or maybe something like "The Pussy Wagon". I would love to hit the streets in a 2010 Pussy Wagon! Wouldn't you?

I heard a commercial for National Tire and Battery that seemed really hell-bent on making you understand that they were an American company. That they were an American company that was *for* Americans and run *by* Americans. American this. American that. Then they said by 3 Yokohama tires and get the 4th one free. Are these people out of their fucking mind? *Yokohama* tires?? All this shit about being an American company and you want people to buy a foreign fucking tire?!? Actually I never took the time to look up if Yokohama was even a foreign company or not. Just in case they're American, I'd rather not know. It's funnier to me that way.

Don't you wish you could solve all the problems in your life with just the push of a button? I don't have any follow up to this. I just thought it would be cool. Sorry.

An actually ad for Rosetta Stone language lessons. *"Do you remember how you learned English? It came to you naturally."* The fuck it did! You were surrounded by it and you *absorbed* it! No language comes to anyone naturally! That's like someone throwing you in the water and saying swimming comes to you naturally. It's either that or drowning! Not much of a choice, dickheads!

Whenever someone says they're traveling, by foot or car, they say they're walking/driving *down* the street. Why is it always 'down'? Not all travel is downhill! You sometimes hear people say they're "going up" to see someone. But that implies a change in altitude as well. "I'm going up to see my folks on Sunday". "Oh, yeah? Where do they live?" "Just down the street." What the fuck?!?

The metric system is very logical. It's neat and organized. Everything between one unit of measure and another is in terms of 10 or a variant thereof. A kilogram is a thousand grams. A millimeter is 1/1000 of a meter. It's clean and tidy. That must be why America refuses to adopt it.

Sometimes you hear that life is a highway. I think there's some truth to that. The problem is mine is loaded with detours, dead ends and potholes the size of moon craters. I think I can come up with a better analogy. *Life is a big, fat, uninvited, clap-ridden, scab-infested dick in the ass.* That seems to fit a little better. In a manner of speaking.

When the fuck did these companies start packing 15 water bottles in a case? What happened to 12? In addition to the standard 6-pack, there are only 2 denominations of beverage casing: 12 and 24. Whose been fucking with the packing machines?? I can see if they're giving me 3 bottles for free. I have no problem getting free shit. But chances are those assholes are charging me for them.

More song lyrics I can do without. There is this Pig and Bitch song. No wait. Sorry. It's Big and Rich. I always mix that up. The song is titled "Comin' to Your City". One of the lyrics in that song is "*then we rolled on into Canton; scared the hell out of Marilyn Manson*". Are these redneck assholes fucking serious?? Have you seen Marilyn Manson lately?!? Do these hillbilly fucks honestly think they're capable of scaring him?? Get fucking lucid! I can't say I know everything there is to know in this world, but if I know anything, it's that you never fuck with a guy with 2 different colored eyes wearing women's lingerie. It's just bad policy!

Here's a good way to cash in on the next Super Bowl. Before the big game, pick either team and have shirts made up that, on the front, declare them the champions. I think better with examples, so let's take the year as of this writing, which would be the Colts and the Saints. Say you chose the Saints as the champions. The moment after the game was over, you could've clean up selling "Saints NFL Champion" shirts right outside the stadium. Now, if in case the Colts had won, all you had to do is have a silk-screen machine ready and on the back of every shirt you'd print "NOT!" and then you would still have sold a shitload of them to Indy fans. It would have been a little more work, but in the end, you still get a sellout.

Just about every grocery store you go to, they have an Express Lane. 10 items or less. 12 items or less. No checks. Whatever. There are many variations, but the principle is the same. What they need to have is a special lane for panicky jackoffs. You know who I'm talking about. The same assholes who, every time there are going to be more than 6 snowflakes landing on the ground, go fucking bananas and buy everything in the fucking store! 16 cases of bottled water. 600 rolls of toilet paper. These stupid fucks have 4 grocery carts full of everything they aren't capable of producing themselves. And it never fails that these cocksuckers get in line 5 seconds before I'm about to check out with my half-gallon of milk, a box of Hamburger Helper and 2 Slim Jims. Can't we have a special line for these douchebags so the rest of us normal, logical people can be spared the agony of having to deal with them?

Here would be a great way to really fuck up the FCC. Make everyday words slang profanity. Not like fish, or baseball, or cookie. I mean common words like 'the'. They'd be going ape shit trying to keep up with that fucking bleeper button!

Yoplait advertises their yogurt sometimes with the line "*May be good for digestion*". That's pretty weak! I *may* start shitting gold doubloons tomorrow but it isn't very fucking likely! The word 'may' should never be used in a commercial. It either does or it doesn't! Take a stand, you pussies!

It's common for young kids to voice their disapproval for something by saying it "sucks" and usually adults won't think anything of it. To me, this is a huge double standard. What do people think the word 'suck' refers to? Sucking a lollipop? Sucking a Slurpie through a straw? No! It means sucking a dick. Felatio! Say it with me Feee-Layyy-Sheeee-Ohhhh! If kids are allowed to make reference to the act of slurping up and down the shaft of a big sweaty cock, the occasional f-bomb should be perfectly acceptable. As long as it's grammatically correct.

You remember how when you were young, you used to eat paste. Or if you didn't, you at least knew someone who did? I'm surprised glue sticks haven't replaced that. Think about it. Same great taste and gooey consistency with none of the mess! Just like those ice cream sherbet Push-Up treats!

I wonder how it is 'pussy' became a profanity. The original full reference to a feline is *pussycat*. At some point 'cat' was chosen for the animal and 'pussy' was chosen for the 'vagina'. Who made this decision? And why was I not consulted? If anyone knows about profanity, it's me. Next decision like this that's made, I want to know about it. It's only right.